Just Between Ourselves

A Play

ALAN AYCKBOURN

SAMUEL FRENCH

LONDON
NEW YORK TORONTO SYDNEY HOLLYWOOD

© 1978 by Redburn Productions Ltd

This play is fully protected under the Copyright Laws of the British Commonwealth of Nations, the United States of America and all countries of the Berne and Universal Copyright Conventions.

All rights, including Stage, Motion Picture, Radio, Television, Public Reading, and Translation into Foreign Languages, are strictly reserved.

No part of this publication may lawfully be transmitted, stored in a retrieval system, or reproduced in any form or by any means, electronic, mechanical, photocopying, manuscript, typescript, recording, or otherwise, without the prior permission of the copyright owners.

Rights of Performance by Amateurs are controlled by SAMUEL FRENCH LTD, 26 SOUTHAMPTON STREET, LONDON WC2E 7JE, and they, or their authorized agents, issue licences to amateurs on payment of a fee. **It is an infringement of the Copyright to give any performance or public reading of the play before the fee has been paid and the licence issued.**

Licences are issued subject to the understanding that it shall be made clear in all advertising matter that the audience will witness an amateur performance; that the names of the authors of the plays shall be included on all announcements and on all programmes; and that the integrity of the author's work will be preserved.

The Royalty Fee indicated below is subject to contract and subject to variation at the sole discretion of Samuel French Ltd

    Basic fee for each and every
    performance by amateurs   **Code M**
    in the British Isles

In Theatres or Halls seating Six Hundred or more the fee will be subject to negotiation.

In Territories Overseas the fee quoted above may not apply. A fee will be quoted on application to our local authorized agent, or if there is no such agent, on application to Samuel French Ltd, London.

The Professional Rights in this play are controlled by Margaret Ramsay Ltd, 14a Goodwin's Court, St Martin's Lane, London WC2

The publication of this play does not imply that it is necessarily available for performance by amateurs or professionals, either in the British Isles or Overseas. Amateurs and professionals considering a production are strongly advised in their own interests to apply to the appropriate agents for consent before starting rehearsals or booking a theatre or hall.

ISBN 573 11212 6

Just Between Ourselves

First presented in London by Michael Codron at the Queen's Theatre, on 22nd April 1977, with the following cast of characters:

Dennis   Colin Blakely
Vera, his wife   Rosemary Leach
Neil   Michael Gambon
Marjorie, Dennis's mother   Constance Chapman
Pam, Neil's wife   Stephanie Turner

The play directed by Alan Strachan

The action takes place in the garage and pathway of Dennis's home

ACT I   Scene 1   February, Saturday around noon
        Scene 2   May, Saturday afternoon
ACT II Scene 1   October, Saturday evening
        Scene 2   January, Saturday morning

Time—the present.

The publication of this play in French's Acting Edition must not be taken to imply that it is available for performance. To avoid possible infringement of the copyright please read the fee notice very carefully.

ACT I

Scene 1

A garage attached to a medium-price executive house on a private estate, belonging to Dennis and Vera. February

Our view is of one side of the house, and looking into the garage through its side wall. The downstage wall, and one end wall, of the garage are constructed as an open framework. The "up-and-over" garage door remains closed throughout the action. An L-shaped workbench runs round one corner of the garage and about half-way along the downstage wall. It is littered untidily with tools, etc., and the whole place is filled with the usual garage junk, boxes, coils of rope, garden chairs, etc. In the midst of this, sideways on, a small popular car, at least seven years old, stands neglected. In the upstage wall of the garage is a grimy window with crowded shelves on either side. There is a dilapidated, flat-topped oil stove below the car, and a wooden box on the floor above the car to facilitate the actors being seen when they are behind it. Below the garage a paved walkway runs the full width of the stage—widening out to a "sitting area"—with a garden gate leading off at the corner. Opposite the "up-and-over" door a small door, opening outwards, leads across a small dustbin yard to the back door of the house. The dustbin is below the house door. Between the wall of the house and the garage, above the dustbin yard, there is a fairly high fence with a holly tree above it. On either side of the gate there are flower-beds with small ornamental trees and one or two withered shrubs. There is a square, brick flower-tub with a dead geranium plant (which is exchanged for a flowering geranium in the summer scene) situated in the centre of the downstage wall of the garage

Dennis, *in his forties, is busy at his workbench. He is prodding at an electric kettle with a screwdriver muttering to himself. After a moment,* **Vera**, *his wife a few years younger, emerges from the back door of the house. She is followed by* **Neil**, *in his late thirties and smartly dressed in contrast to* **Dennis** *who has on his week-end clothes*

Dennis (*frowning at the kettle*) That goes in there—and then that one goes—through there to that one—which should join up with the other one. In which case ...

Vera (*knocking gently on the garage door*) Dennis—Dennis.

Dennis (*still absorbed*) But in that case, that one—should be joined to that one ... (*calling*) Hallo—(*returning to the kettle*)—unless that's the earth. In which case, it's that one.

Vera (*struggling with the door, trying to open it*) Dennis.

Dennis Come in. (*Back to the kettle*) On the other hand, if that's the earth which one is the live one ... ?

Vera Dennis dear, can you open the door for me please. It's stuck again.
Dennis Hang on, hang on, hang on. Live—earth—neutral.
Vera (*to Neil apologetically*) It's always sticking.
Neil Ah.
Dennis Earth, neutral, live.
Vera My husband's going to fix it as soon as he has a moment but ... Dennis dear.
Dennis (*backing towards the door keeping his eyes fixed on the kettle*) Right. In which case, if that's the earth it goes in there ... Hang on—not in there—right. Stand back.
Vera (*to Neil*) Stand back.

Vera and Neil back from the garage door. Dennis heaves against it, and it flies open

Dennis I'll tell you one thing, the fellow who invented the electric kettle ... (*Seeing Neil*) Ah. Afternoon.
Neil Good afternoon.
Vera Dennis dear, this gentleman's come to look at the car.
Dennis At the car?
Vera Mr ... Sorry, I've forgotten your name.
Neil Mr Andrews.
Dennis Pleased to meet you, Mr Andrews, come in, come in.
Neil Thank you.
Vera This is my husband, Mr Crowthorne.
Neil (*shaking hands with Dennis*) How do you do?
Dennis Excuse the jumble. The place is due for a spring clean. Amazing what you collect.
Neil Yes, yes.
Dennis Amazing. I mean, where does it all come from. Just look at it. I mean, where does it all come from.
Neil Yes, yes. Accumulates.
Dennis Accumulates. That's the word, accumulates.
Vera How's my kettle?
Dennis Coming along, coming along.
Vera It just wasn't heating up at all. Your mother's making tea in a saucepan.
Dennis Well, I'll tell you, my love, I'll give you a little tip shall I. A little tip when you're next using an electric kettle. They work far better when you don't keep slinging them on the floor.
Vera I couldn't help it. I just caught it with my elbow.
Dennis (*to Neil, laughing*) Caught it with her elbow.

Neil smiles

If I told you, Mr Andrews, the things my wife had caught with her elbow ...
Vera (*shy and embarrassed*) All right.
Dennis You would not believe it, Mr Andrews, cups, saucers, dinner plates, radio sets ...
Neil Really.
Dennis Whole tray of glasses.

Act I Scene 1

Vera Dennis ...
Dennis And that's just for this month. You ever want a demolition job doing, Mr Andrews, she's your woman. (*He laughs*)

Neil joins in half-heartedly. Vera less so still

    Elbows going away like pistons ...
Neil Well, I suppose we all tend to—occasionally.
Dennis Yes, quite (*Hugging Vera*) I was only joking, love, only joking. I'm always pulling her leg, aren't I, love? Eh? I'll have it fixed in a jiffy. I'll bring it in.
Vera Right. I'll make you both some tea when the saucepan's boiled. (*She moves to the door then turns back to Neil*) Do you take sugar, Mr ...
Neil No, thank you. Unfortunately. I'm afraid I'm unable to take it.
Vera Right then. (*She turns to leave*)

Marjorie, a woman in her sixties, comes out of the back-door

Marjorie Vera dear, there's a terrible smell of gas ...
Vera All right, Mother, I'm coming. Excuse me.
Marjorie I'm sure this stove still isn't right.
Dennis Check the pilot light, Vee. Check it hasn't blown out.
Marjorie It hasn't been right since I gave it that thorough clean.
Vera All right, Mother, all right.
Dennis Vee'll see to it, Mother.

Vera and Marjorie go back into the house

    My mother, you met my mother?
Neil Yes, I met her on the way through to ...
Dennis Sixty-six.
Neil What?
Dennis Sixty-six years old.
Neil Really?
Dennis Not bad for sixty-six.
Neil No, no.
Dennis It's the pilot light, you see. It's in a cross draught. It's very badly sited that stove. They should never have put it there. I'm planning to move it. Right, now. You've come about the car, haven't you?
Neil That's right.
Dennis Well, there she is. Have a look for yourself. That's the one. (*He pushes the rubbish off the bonnet*)
Neil Ah.
Dennis Now, I'll tell you a little bit about it, shall I? Bit of history. Number One, it's not my car. It's the wife's. However, now before you say—ah-ha, woman driver—she's been very careful with it. Never had a single accident in it touch wood. Well I mean, look you can see hardly a scratch on it. Considering the age. To be perfectly honest, just between ourselves, she's

a better driver than me—when she puts her mind to it. I mean, look—considering it's, what now—seven—nearly eight years old. Just look for yourself at that bodywork.

Neil Yes, yes.

Dennis I bought it four years ago for her. It was then as good as new—virtually. Three years old and as good as new it was.

Neil It looks very good.

Dennis It is really, amazingly good.

Neil I suppose being under cover ...

Dennis Ah yes, well, quite. As I was just about to say, being under cover as it is.

Neil Important.

Dennis Vital. Vital to keep a car under cover. I mean, frankly that's why we want to get rid of it. I want to get my own car under cover. I don't know if you saw it when you were coming in, parked just out there on the road.

Neil Yes, I think I ...

Dennis It's doing it no good at all. It's an urgent priority to get that car under cover. You've got a garage, I take it?

Neil No.

Dennis Ah. Well, when I say that, with a car like this one, it's not as vital as with some cars. I mean, this one—(*he slaps the bonnet*)—this is a very, very sturdy vehicle indeed. As a matter of fact, they're not even making them any more. Not this particular model. They took up too much raw material. They're not economic to make. There's a lot of raw material in this. Mind you, there's no problem with parts. They're still making the parts, they're just not making the cars. Not that you'll ever need a part. We've never needed a part not in four years. No, as a matter of fact, I'll let you into a little secret. This car has barely been out of this garage in six months.

Neil Really?

Dennis Barely been out. As a matter of fact, frankly, just between ourselves, the wife's had a few, what shall I say, health worries and she hasn't really been up to driving.

Neil Oh, I'm sorry to ...

Dennis Oh, she's better now. She's very much better now. But she's gone off driving altogether. You can see, look—look at that clock there—I'll be surprised if it's done fifty thousand. (*Peering in*) Here we are.

Neil also peers in

Fifty-five thousand two hundred and fifty two miles—well, fifty-five, fifty thousand, round about that figure.

Neil Amazing.

Dennis Peanuts for a car like this. It's hardly run in.

Neil Right.

Dennis Have a look for yourself anyway. Feel free.

Neil Thanks.

Neil wanders round the car aimlessly; Dennis follows him

Dennis I'd let you have a test drive in it now but—actually it's a bit embarrass-

Act I Scene 1

ing—the up and over door there, you see it's gone and jammed itself somehow, can't get it open at all. Still that's my next job.
Neil Oh. Well, it'll be important, won't it to ...
Dennis Oh, surely surely. Wouldn't expect you to consider it without a run around. Still you can have a preliminary look. See if it's the sort of thing you're looking for.
Neil Oh yes.
Dennis Here. We can have a butchers at the business end. Just a tick. (*He releases the bonnet*) There she is.
Neil Oh yes. (*He looks at the engine*)
Dennis Not bad, eh?
Neil No.
Dennis Economic.
Neil Really.
Dennis Very smooth runner.
Neil Ah.
Dennis I'll tell you what I can do for you, I can turn it over for you. Then you can hear the sound. (*He opens the door and gets into the driver's seat*)
Neil Oh well, that's ...
Dennis Keys are in it, I think—yes, right. I can't run it for too long, not in an enclosed space, you understand but—bit of choke—right—stand by for blast off.

Neil stands by the car, holding the bonnet open. The engine turns over but fails to start

She'll be a little bit cold.

The engine fails to start again

Come along, my beauty. She's been standing, you see.

Dennis tries again. It fails to start

Come on, come on, you bastard.

The engine turns and starts to fire. Neil keeps hold of the bonnet, shaking it gently to denote engine vibration

There we are. (*He climbs out of the car and joins Neil*) Listen to that. Purring like a kitten.
Neil Beg your pardon?
Dennis (*yelling above the din*) That's with the bonnet open, of course.
Neil Yes.

They stand and survey the turning engine. After a moment it starts to misfire. Dennis pushes against the side of the car to keep it going. The engine peters out. Silence

Dennis Battery'll be a little flat, I expect.
Neil Probably.
Dennis Once it's had a bit of a run round. Desperately needs a good run. Do you do a lot of driving? (*He turns off the ignition*)

Neil No. As a matter of fact, I don't drive at all.
Dennis Eh? (*straightens up D/S of window, look at Neil*)
Neil No, I never got round to learning. My wife drives.
Dennis Oh, it's for your wife then, is it?
Neil That's right.
Dennis Oh I see, I see. Surprise, is it?
Neil That sort of thing, yes.
Dennis Surprise. That's nice. That's nice. Does she suspect? Does she know where you are today then?
Neil Yes.
Dennis Ah.
Neil She's here as well.
Dennis Here?
Neil I left here in your front room, talking to your mother.
Dennis Well, doesn't she want to come and have a look? Since she's here.
Neil No, I don't think so.
Dennis Well, of course it's an ideal woman's car. Not too big, you see. And it's got the radio. That comes with it, of course. It's a good radio. (*He opens the car door, gets in, and turns the radio on*)

There is a buzzing noise. Dennis turns it off quickly

    It won't work of course, not while it's in the garage. And then you've got your mirrors behind the sun visors here.
Neil (*looking in the car*) Oh yes.
Dennis Little touches like that. Sort of thing a woman looks for.
Neil Handy.
Dennis (*getting out of the car*) Oh yes. Funny her coming all this way with you and then not wanting to see it for herself.
Neil We hadn't far to come.
Dennis She prefers to leave it to the expert, does she?
Neil Oh, I'm not an expert. No, I was going to have this car delivered for her this morning from another man.
Dennis Ah.
Neil Only he let me down at the last minute.
Dennis It's undersealed, you see. Have a look underneath, see. (*He looks underneath the car*)
Neil (*bending down to look*) He sold this car of his to somebody else. Phoned me late last night. I didn't want to let her down. Oh yes, very nice.
Dennis Important to underseal.
Neil So I had to phone round in a hurry this morning. (*He rises, and suffers a mild spasm of indigestion*) Excuse me.
Dennis (*rising*) You all right?
Neil Oh yes. Just a touch of indigestion.
Dennis Oh dear. Been living it up, have you?
Neil No, no. I only get it when I bend down. Nothing serious.
Dennis That's odd. Sure it's indigestion?
Neil I think it is.
Dennis Could be something else.

Act I Scene 1

Neil Could it?
Dennis Possibly. I'd get it looked at, if I were you.
Neil Think so?
Dennis No harm. I mean, nine times out of ten you're probably right it's indigestion but the stomach's a peculiar thing.
Neil Is it?
Dennis Yes. I've had experience with stomachs.
Neil Have you?
Dennis (*closing the bonnet*) Better safe than sorry.
Neil Anyway this chap let me down, you see, at the last minute. So I went through the small ads again this morning and, er, there was your advert. So I spoke to your wife.
Dennis I see, yes.
Neil I didn't want to disappoint her. Birthday, you see.
Dennis Birthday? It's your wife's birthday then?
Neil Yes.
Dennis Today?
Neil Yes.
Dennis Good heavens above. Pisces, eh?
Neil What?
Dennis Her star sign. Pisces.
Neil Oh yes.
Dennis You better keep an eye on her, mate.
Neil How do you mean?
Dennis They can get very moody can Pisces. Very moody brooding people. Unless you keep a very close watch on them. What sign are you, as a matter of interest?
Neil Er well, Scorpio I think.
Dennis (*with a yell*) Scorpio.
Neil Yes.
Dennis Living with a Pisces.
Neil Yes.
Dennis Good grief.
Neil Is that bad?
Dennis Perfect, perfect. Made for each other. Couldn't be better.
Neil Oh, good.
Dennis You don't look like a Scorpio. My mother's a Scorpio. She's a typical Scorpio. I mean, she's got the Scorpio bone structure. But you don't look a bit like a Scorpio. What date are you?
Neil Twenty-eighth of October.
Dennis (*with another wild yell*) Twenty-eighth of October! I don't believe it. I do not believe it.
Neil Eh?
Dennis You won't believe this. You will not believe this. You were born on exactly the same day as my mother.
Neil Oh.
Dennis Exactly the same day. Exactly the same day.
Neil Coincidence.

Dennis This was meant. I'm sure it was meant. It's extraordinary.
Neil Yes, yes it is.
Dennis Ah, well. Scorpio, eh? I'll have to keep an eye on you.
Neil Really.
Dennis Oh yes. Very deep waters, Scorpio. Very deep, secretive, scheming and occasionally, I regret to say, devious.
Neil Oh, well. I'll watch it then.
Dennis What a coincidence. Incredible. You don't have to worry about me though. I'm a Taurus.
Neil Oh good.

Vera comes out from the kitchen with two cups of tea

Vera Dennis.
Dennis Ah ha. That sounds like an Aquarius. The water bearer bringing the tea. (*He wrenches open the door*)
Vera Here's your tea.
Dennis Vee, now you won't believe this, Vee, we have just discovered that Mr Andrews here has exactly the same birth date as Mother. Isn't that extraordinary?
Vera Oh, coincidence.
Dennis To the day. Both Scorpios. Exactly the same date.
Vera Not the same year though
Dennis Same year? Oh yes, rather. Exactly the same year. Mr Andrews here will be sixty-seven next birthday, won't you, Mr Andrews?
Vera No, I said not the same ...
Dennis Same year. Get on with you. Same year. (*He hugs her*)
Vera Careful. I'll drop them.
Dennis Well, it won't be the first time.
Vera Dennis ...
Dennis Aquarius. You can tell, can't you? Typical bloody dopey Aquarius. Aren't you, my love?
Vera Sugar's in it, Mr Andrews. (*She hands Neil his tea*)
Neil Oh. Is it? Thank you.

Vera hands Dennis his tea

Dennis You given Mrs Andrews some tea?
Vera Yes, she's talking to Mother.
Dennis Well, I don't know about talking to Mother. I think she ought to be out here with me and Mr—look, can I call you by your Christian name, all this Mr this and Mr that.
Neil Neil.
Dennis Neil. Right, I'm Dennis. This is Vera. Vee she prefers.
Neil How do you do.
Dennis Well, don't you think we ought to ask er—your wife ...
Neil Pam.
Dennis Pam—Brian's wife's called Pam, isn't she?
Vera Yes.

Act I Scene 1

Dennis Ask Pam out here. After all it's her present. I mean, assuming you're still interested.
Neil Yes. It's just that I don't think she's ...
Vera Oh, is the car for your wife?
Neil Yes.
Vera Oh I see. It's very good. It's a nice little car. I've had very little trouble with it.
Dennis Very little? Now be truthful, Vee, you've had no trouble. Be truthful.
Vera It did break down that once on the ring road.
Dennis Petrol. That was petrol.
Vera Oh yes.
Dennis It's not the car's fault if you don't put petrol in it, is it? Not the car's fault. Whose fault is it if there's no petrol in it?
Vera Yes, all right.
Dennis Whose fault?
Vera Yes, all right, Dennis.
Dennis It's little Vee's fault. Vee's fault that's whose it is. I tell you, Neil, I don't know if your wife's the same but if you do give her a car watch her like a hawk. She'll never put petrol in it. She'll never put water in it. She'll never do the tyres and as for oil—well, they've never heard of oil except on salads. Eh?

Neil laughs. A token laugh

Except on salads, eh? (*He leans on the front wing, helpless with laughter*)
Vera Shall I fetch Pam in here?
Dennis Yes, fetch her in, Vee, fetch her in. Let her have a look at it.
Neil I don't think she's that bothered actually.
Dennis Of course she's bothered. What is it, her first car is it?
Neil No, she had one a long time ago before we were married.
Dennis Well, nearly her first car. Her first car for some time. She'll want to see what she's getting. My God, if I was getting my first car, I'd be ...
Vera Yes all right, I'll fetch her. Drink your tea, Mr—Neil. (*She starts to go*)
Neil Thank you.
Vera Mother burnt herself on that saucepan, Dennis.
Dennis First-aid tin, top shelf over the boiler.
Vera I know, I have already. She says it's the wrong stuff.

Vera goes into the house

Dennis Now, listen. (*He goes to the door, looks through, then comes back*) We must do this thing properly. When Pam comes through the door everything must be right. She comes in the door, what does she see? She sees the car ...

Neil gives a slight belch

You all right?
Neil Yes, fine. I seem to have got the tea with the sugar in.
Dennis What? (*He takes a swig of his own*) Here have this one. That's hardly got any sugar in at all.

They exchange cups. Dennis turns way, appraising the situation. Neil takes a sip of Dennis's tea and reacts unfavourably

She comes in, she sees the car and, how about if you were sitting behind the wheel, no, in the passenger seat, that's it, in the passenger seat and as soon as she sees you, you say to her—happy birthday, my darling Pam or whatever you usually call her, dearest, dear, how would you like this for your birthday? (*He puts his cup on the bench*)

Neil Well, I don't think she's the sort of person who goes for ...

Dennis Look, Neil, there is not a woman who has yet been born who does not respond to a romantic gesture. Come on, man, where's your romance?

Neil Do you mind if I leave this tea?

Dennis Is that too sweet as well?

Neil It's even sweeter.

Dennis It's all right. I'll drink them both. I'll drink them both.

Neil puts his cup on the oil stove

Vera comes out of the house with Pam, a woman in her middle to late thirties

Vera They're just out here.

Dennis Here they come. Here they come. Quick get in the car, quick, quick, quick.

Dennis pushes Neil to the car so that he can get into the passenger seat, then leans against the garage door until Neil is in position

Vera (*tugging at the door handle*) Dennis. Dennis. Can you let us in?

Dennis Just a minute. Just a minute. (*He turns to Neil with a thumbs-up gesture*)

Vera Stand back.

Pam and Vera stand back just in time: Dennis opens the door

Dennis Come in. Come in. (*He backs to the car with arms outstretched*)

Pam enters slowly, sees Neil sitting in the car and stares at him

Neil Hallo. (*He looks out of the passenger window*)

Pam Hallo.

Dennis (*gesticulating wildly to Neil*) Go on.

Pam What are you doing?

Neil Er—just looking at the car.

Pam Oh. (*She moves slowly to the car, kicks the wheel, then moves below it*)

Neil (*looking out of the window*) What do you think?

Pam I said, it's up to you.

Neil Yes, I know but—I mean you're going to be driving it. (*He gets out of the car*)

Pam As long as it goes.

Vera Oh it goes. It did go anyway.

Dennis Still goes.

Act I Scene 1   11

Neil What do you think?
Pam Well.
Neil Yes.
Dennis (*in another of his fierce undertones*) Show her the radio. And the—(*he gesticulates*)—the mirror.
Neil (*to Pam in an undertone, moving away a little*) What do you think?
Pam (*likewise*) What's he asking?
Neil Four hundred.
Dennis Four hundred.
Pam (*moving further away from Dennis*) It's not worth four hundred.
Neil I don't know.
Pam It's never worth four hundred. Offer him three fifty.
Neil Oh, you know I can't ...
Pam Three fifty. Settle for three seventy-five. He'd still be doing us.
Neil Oh, you know I can't do that sort of thing. You know I—
Pam Yes, I know you. (*To Dennis*) How long have you had it?
Dennis Three and a hal ...
Vera Four years.
Dennis Nearly four years. (*He glares at Vera*)
Vera Served me very well. Nice little car.
Dennis (*bounding forward unable to restrain himself*) Look, you see. It's got the mirror here.
Pam Oh yes, so it has.

Neil and Pam move a little away

Neil Well, do you want it?
Pam It's nothing to do with me, love, it's your money.
Neil No, it's our money.
Pam Yours. You wanted to get a car. I didn't ask for one.
Neil But you did say you'd like one, didn't you? You said ...
Pam I said nothing of the sort.
Neil You said ...
Pam I have not said a single word on the subject. Not a word. It's entirely up to you.
Neil I just thought you'd—that you could get out occasionally.
Pam When am I going to get out occasionally?
Neil I just thought ...
Pam Where the hell am I supposed to be going?
Neil I simply thought you'd ...
Pam It's your money, love. If you want a car, you buy one.
Dennis Oh, by the way, just a point of interest. It is taxed for another three months. I forgot to mention that.
Neil Yes, well I—I think we'll leave it for now if you don't mind.
Dennis Leave it?
Neil Just for the time being. It's a bit difficult deciding in a rush, you know. Till we've had a chance of a run out in it. You know.
Dennis Ah. Now, I'll have that garage door fixed in the next twenty-four hours.

Vera Oh do, please. It's been like that for months.
Neil It's a bit difficult to decide just on the spur of the moment. It may be just a bit more than we were prepared to ...
Dennis Well, I said four hundred. Because that's the fair price but I'll take a near offer. Three seventy-five?
Neil No, not just at the ...
Dennis Three sixty-five. There you are. Now I'm giving it away. Three sixty-five.
Neil No. Perhaps I could pop back sometime.
Dennis Yes, you're welcome to do that. But I must warn you I have one or two interested people.
Pam Yes, I'm sure.
Dennis Yes. Well. Feel free to pop back.
Neil Thank you. (*He has another spasm of indigestion*) Excuse me.
Pam Don't do that.
Neil I can't help it.
Pam Take one of your tablets.
Neil I left them at home.
Pam Oh God.
Vera Anything the matter?
Pam Heaven knows.
Neil No, no. Just a touch of indigestion I suffer occasionally.
Vera Oh dear. Would you like some bicarb?
Neil No, no, that's ...
Vera No, we've got some milk of magnesia somewhere.
Neil No, no thank you. I have my own special tablets.
Vera Oh I see.
Dennis I'd have a check up if I were you.
Vera Can be nasty, indigestion.
Dennis Supposing it is indigestion.
Vera Oh yes, supposing it is.
Neil Yes, well, thank you very much.
Dennis Not at all. We're always open.
Neil Leave you to get on with your kettle.
Dennis Yes, yes.
Vera Have you far to go?
Pam No, not far.
Neil Easterly Road.
Vera Oh, Easterly Road. We used to live just off Easterly Road didn't we, Dennis?
Dennis That's right.
Vera One of the new houses, is it?
Pam No, the old ones.
Neil On the left just at the top.
Vera Oh, I know them, yes. In that little block on its own. Didn't Mrs—er—whatever's her name—didn't she live up there, Dennis?
Dennis I didn't know they were still there, those places.
Pam Just about.

Act I Scene 1

Vera What was her name, Dennis? She used to live there with her son who was a bit funny. You know, peculiar.
Dennis I thought those places were scheduled to come down.
Neil I hope not. We're still paying for ours.
Dennis I thought I read that somewhere.
Vera Mrs—er ...
Dennis For road widening.
Neil We've never heard anything about it, have we?
Pam That's hardly surprising.
Vera Mrs—um ...
Dennis Yes, road widening. I'm sure it was that end of Easterly Road.
Neil Just be our luck wouldn't it?
Pam Well, we must get on.
Vera Mrs Mandelsham. That was her name. Mrs Mandelsham.
Neil Mrs Mandelsham?
Vera Do you know her?
Pam She's my mother.
Neil Pam's mother. Living with us now.
Vera Good gracious. Did you hear that, Dennis?
Dennis Yes, yes.
Vera Then you must be Pamela Mandelsham.
Pam I was.
Vera Well. Isn't that extraordinary? We used to know Mrs Mandelsham ever so well. Do you remember, Dennis? The nice woman with the cakes.
Dennis With the cakes, that's right.
Vera Of course, you weren't there when we were.
Pam No, I was working away. I came back when I married Neil.
Vera Of course we knew your brother. Graham, wasn't it?
Pam Adam.
Vera Adam. That's right. How is he?
Pam Still a bit peculiar. He got married and moved to Liverpool. Haven't seen him for ages. Got masses of kids.
Vera Oh well, fancy that. And your mother? How is she? Keeping well?
Pam Fine.
Neil Yes.
Pam She's baby-sitting for us.
Neil She's well. She's very well indeed.
Vera Well, just fancy that. You must come round again. Bring your mother.
Pam Yes. We must.
Vera She made those wonderful cakes, didn't she, Dennis? She was always trying to teach me. I'd like to see her again.
Pam Yes.
Dennis Yes.
Neil Yes.

A pause

Pam Well. We better get on with it. Get Darren his tea.
Vera Oh yes. Let me ... (*She leads the way to the garage door*)

Pam follows

Neil Well, good-bye. Thanks very much again.

Neil and Dennis move towards the garage door together

Dennis Not at all, Neil. As I say, look in any time. If you want a second look at this thing—just barge in. You're always welcome.
Neil Thanks.
Dennis Good-bye, Pam.
Pam 'Bye.
Dennis Happy birthday.

They all stop between the garage and house doors

Vera Oh yes, happy birthday. Whose birthday is it?
Dennis Hers. Pam's. It's Pam's birthday.
Vera Oh, happy birthday.

Marjorie emerges from the house

Marjorie I'm going to have to leave the potatoes to you, Vera.
Vera Oh, Mother. You shouldn't have started on that yet. It's far too early.
Marjorie I've been struggling with that little knife of yours.
Vera We're not having dinner for hours.
Dennis Go on, Mother, you clear off out of it. Let the Queen back in her kitchen.
Marjorie It's all very well. We've been having our meals later and later.
Dennis 'Bye.
Neil 'Bye. (*He turns to shake hands with Dennis*)

Vera, Pam and Neil go into the house

Dennis goes into his garage and starts working on the kettle with a screwdriver

Dennis Now then. Where were we? This little one comes up here and joins up with this one. Now which did we say was the earth?

Marjorie comes from the house and into the garage

Marjorie Come on then. Let's have your cups.
Dennis Help yourself.
Marjorie That's if I can carry them.
Dennis Your hands bad again?
Marjorie Not so good today. (*She picks up the cup from the bench*)
Dennis Oh dear. Must be the weather.
Marjorie No, it's not the weather. I'm afraid it's age, Dennis. It's what happens when you get old, I'm afraid. Everything just stops working bit by bit. I'm afraid you'll soon find that out for yourself. (*She picks up the cup from the oil stove*)
Dennis (*unperturbed*) Probably will, Mother, yes.

Act I Scene 1

Marjorie Someone hasn't drunk his tea.
Dennis He didn't take sugar.
Marjorie Oh. That was Vera. Did you sell the car?
Dennis No.
Marjorie No, I was talking to the woman. She didn't seem very keen. I don't think she wanted a car anyway. It was him. I told her. I said you don't want a car. They're more trouble than they're worth. (*She puts the cups on the bench, turning slightly from Dennis*)
Dennis (*raising his fist, threatening Marjorie*) You told her that, did you?

Marjorie turns to Dennis, who relaxes his fist and scratches his head

Marjorie Well, I mean, look at Vera. She's had this car for years. She never drives it. I doubt if she's driven it once this year.
Dennis Ah well, in Vera's case—you know.
Marjorie You want to keep more of an eye on her, Dennis.
Dennis How do you mean?
Marjorie She's a sick girl. She's not well if you ask me.
Dennis No, she's better now, Mother. She's much better.
Marjorie Now, don't let her fool you, Dennis. She's not a bit better. You don't get better. Not from that. When it's up here, in your head, it's there for good.
Dennis She seems all right to me.
Marjorie I've got a feeling she's got what our Joan had. God rest her soul.
Dennis Oh come on, Mother, Auntie Joan went right round the bloody bend.
Marjorie Yes, I know. I nursed her. And she started just like Vera.
Dennis The doctor said she was better.
Marjorie Did he? Well.
Dennis Well, nearly better anyway. That was months ago.
Marjorie When she dropped that kettle, I was watching her closely. She just burst into tears, you know.
Dennis Not surprised. So did I. Nearly brand new this is. No, mother, if there's anything wrong with Vera it's because she's in a rut. She needs cheering up. Taking out of herself. She takes life too seriously. For that matter, both of you do.
Marjorie (*wiping the top of the oil stove and sitting on it*) Well, Dennis, that might be your solution but I can tell you from my experience it is not the solution for Vera. Nor for me, I'm afraid. Nor was it for Auntie Joan, God rest her soul. I know they say laughter's a great tonic but there are some things it can't heal. You can't laugh everything off, Dennis.
Dennis I know that. I . . .
Marjorie I've certainly never been able to. And nor was your father able to. I sometimes wish you took after your father, Dennis, I really do. Not in all ways but in some things. You could do well to follow him.
Dennis How do you mean?
Marjorie Well, for one thing he didn't try and laugh everything off. He had a deep and wonderful understanding of suffering. In fact, on occasions one could have said too much so. I think by the end, he had taken on everyone's suffering.

Dennis He was a miserable old sod when he died.
Marjorie And another thing your father always did. He always kept his garage tidy. He wouldn't have left it in this state. (*Rising*) How do you ever find anything?
Dennis I can find things, Mother, don't go on.
Marjorie Look at his tools, Dennis. Look at your father's tools. They're all over the place. It would have broken his heart to see them. Why don't you do what he did. Make yourself a proper rack for your tools screwed in the wall. He had little clips, you see. He had his chisels and his screwdrivers and all his hammers ...
Dennis I know. I know.
Marjorie And then on his bench itself, up one end he had all his little tins with his screws and nails and so forth. And he had them all labelled, you see. So whenever he wanted a little nail or a screw, he could just put his hand straight on it.
Dennis Yes, I know, Mother, I was there.
Marjorie No, I remember saving you some tins, Dennis. (*Looking around*) The ones I had my cough sweets in. What did you do with those?
Dennis I don't know (*Indicating a pile of rubbish*) They're under that lot somewhere. I haven't got time, Mother, to start putting things in tins. If I want a nail, there's a nail. I bang it in and that's that. If I can't find a nail, I use a screw. And if I can't find a screw, I don't bother.
Marjorie It'd break his heart in two to see it. Do you remember him working out there in his garage till all hours? Hammering away, making little things. Always beautifully finished. Do you remember his pipe rack?
Dennis Yes. Tremendous. It was a classic among pipe racks. (*He applies himself with fresh fury to the kettle*)
Marjorie He cut that with such care. Do you remember, Dennis? In fretwork, wasn't it? And he cut the letters out in fretwork as well. Pipes. PIPES across the top.
Dennis (*muttering*) In case he forgot what it was for.
Marjorie That gave him more pleasure than anything. Till his eyesight went. Then he could hardly find his way to the garage at all, poor soul. Let alone his fretwork. Ah well, that's age, Dennis, that's age.
Dennis True. True. There's your kettle.
Marjorie (*taking the kettle*) It's not going to blow up, is it?
Dennis I've arranged it so it does.
Marjorie You're not very good at electrics. I'm still having trouble with that bedside light.
Dennis I've told you it's perfectly safe. The switch may be slightly faulty but it's perfectly safe.
Marjorie It's not the switch I'm worried about. The whole thing keeps falling out of its bottle. I had a lighted bulb in bed with me the other night.
Dennis I'll have another look at it.
Marjorie I daren't turn it on at all.

Vera comes out from the house and goes to the garage

Act I Scene 1

Vera Mother, you left the saucepan on with no water in it.

Dennis laughs and shakes a finger at Marjorie

Marjorie No, that wasn't me, Vera. It wasn't me.
Vera You made the tea. I haven't been near it.
Marjorie I may be getting old, Vera, but I wouldn't be stupid enough to put an empty saucepan back on a lighted gas. I'm not that old, Vera.
Dennis Now then, girls.
Vera Well, it doesn't matter.
Marjorie I thank God that my mind is still perfectly clear. (*She picks up the cups*)
Vera What do you mean?
Dennis Yes, well as soon as it starts to go I'll send for the van, Mother, don't worry.
Marjorie (*speaking confidentially*) No, don't joke about it, Dennis, don't joke. It's only too true. Vera, could you carry these for me? I'm frightened I'll drop them. (*She gives Vera the kettle and both cups*)
Dennis Well, don't give them to Vee.
Marjorie Can you manage?
Vera Yes, I can manage.
Dennis I suppose I'll be mending that again in a minute.
Vera Don't keep on, Dennis love.
Dennis Sorry. Sorry...
Marjorie Now don't tease her, Dennis. You're always teasing the girl. No wonder she's in a state.
Vera I'm not in a state. I'm perfectly all right.
Dennis She's all right now, Mother, don't keep on.
Vera Will you be out here much longer, dear?
Dennis Why?
Vera Oh, no reason. I've had the fire on in the front room. It's very cosy.
Dennis Lovely. Right.
Vera Fancy that woman being Mrs Mandelsham's daughter.
Marjorie Was that Mrs Mandelsham's daughter?
Vera Yes.
Marjorie Well, I never. Yes, she does. She looks like her.
Vera Well, slightly.
Marjorie She will do when she's older.
Vera (*going to the garage door and pushing it open with her knee*) Anyway, apparently her brother, you know, the one we all thought was a bit peculiar, well...

Marjorie leans across Vera to help with the door

It's all right, Mother, I can manage—well, he went to Liverpool and... (*A cup falls from its saucer. She attempts to catch it and succeeds in dropping everything*) Oh God in heaven, this door...
Dennis (*roaring with laughter*) There she goes again. What did I tell you.

Vera stands surveying the wreckage. On the brink of tears, unable to cope, she rushes into the house

Marjorie There you are, Dennis, what did I say? What did I say?
Dennis She's all right, Mother.

Marjorie follows Vera into the house

Oh good, grief...

Dennis goes and picks up the kettle, then returns to the garage, whistling cheerfully, and starts tidying up the bench, as—

the CURTAIN *falls*

Scene 2

The same. May, and sunny

Neil is setting up a small garden table round the side of the garage in the "sitting area". After a moment Pam enters from the house carrying a tray of tea-time preliminaries, and moves to the table

Neil Can you manage?
Pam I can manage.
Neil (*testing the table*) I think this is secure.
Pam Any chairs? (*She lays the plates etc. on the table*)
Neil I don't know. I couldn't find any.
Pam Are we all supposed to stand?
Neil You can't find anything in that place. Oh God, are these cucumber?
Pam You don't have to eat them.
Neil Why cucumber?
Pam These are paste. Have the paste.
Neil We could have brought Darren, you know.
Pam Oh no.
Neil He'd have been happy enough, playing out here. He couldn't come to any harm.
Pam I'd have been up and down all through tea. If there's something that child can get his hands on that he shouldn't do, he does.
Neil I don't know. He's ...
Pam You don't know. That's just the point. You're out all day, aren't you.
Neil No, what I'm saying—
Pam I'm with him, remember. All day. (*She leans the tray against the table*) Every day.

Neil mooches about

Neil (*after a moment*) If you'd let me buy that car, you could've ...
Pam What was I supposed to do with it? Stick Darren in the boot and just drive off.

Act I Scene 2

Neil No. Your mother would have looked after him. You could've gone off for the odd day.
Pam He's getting too much for her now. I can't keep asking her. I trust him more than her.
Neil Well, in the evenings. You could've got to your night classes.
Pam Night classes?
Neil Yes.
Pam I think that was just a lovely dream, Neil. I'm getting too old for that.
Neil Too old? You're only ...
Pam I know how old I am, thank you. I don't need reminding.
Neil I thought you said you wanted to go to night classes.
Pam There's lots of things I want, Neil. But they're not to be are they? If you follow me ...
Neil How do you mean?
Pam You know.
Neil No, what?
Pam You know perfectly well.
Neil What?
Pam I'm not spelling it out, Neil.
Neil Oh.
Pam Yes. That.
Neil Well.
Pam That's what I'm talking about.
Neil Well, I ... (*he picks up a sandwich, embarrassed and chews it*) It's not that I ... well ...
Pam You're eating cucumber.
Neil Oh God.

Vera comes out of the house with a plate of biscuits and cakes

Vera Thank you so much, Pam. If I'd carried it, I'd've probably ... (*She puts the plate on the table*) Oh, chairs. Have we got no chairs, Neil?
Neil I could only find this table.
Vera Oh. Dennis put them away at the end of last year. First time we've brought them out this year. I hope we're doing the right thing today. Still it's very mild.
Pam It's lovely.
Vera Considering it's May.
Neil Yes.
Vera It shouldn't hurt Mother's cold. She's over the worst. Neil, I wonder if you'd be very kind and ask Dennis if he would look out the chairs for us. They're probably tucked away at the back there somewhere. Only he's the only one who'll know where he put them.
Neil Right. (*He has a spasm of indigestion*) Excuse me.
Pam Neil.
Neil Sorry.
Vera He was in the sitting room a moment ago watching the telly.

Neil goes in

Pam Your mother-in-law's better then?
Vera (*setting out cups and saucers*) Oh yes. Over the worst. It's something that's going round, I think. She got up at lunchtime. She wouldn't miss Dennis's birthday tea, that's for sure. She thinks the world of Dennis.
Pam Yes, I gathered.
Vera Won't hear a word against him.
Pam I think Neil's of the same opinion.
Vera Yes, you're right. They're very thick these days, aren't they?
Pam Almost inseparable. Every other evening. I'm just going to have another look at that car, he says, and off he goes.
Vera Well, he's no trouble. Hardly see them. Both shut away in that garage. He keeps Dennis out of mischief.
Pam Yes. (*pause*) I hope you don't mind me saying so, you don't look at all well.
Vera Really? Oh ...
Pam Sorry I don't mean to ...
Vera No, no. I've probably had a bit of a bug as well.
Pam Oh.

Pause

Vera Yes. It's a bit of a bug. Been going around.

Pause

Pam Was it your idea to sell the car?
Vera Er—yes. I think it was, yes. I mean, after all it's my car. Dennis bought it for me but it is mine.
Pam Didn't you use it then?
Vera No, not very much. I—well, if we're going anywhere I go with Dennis. So I go in his car.
Pam But you go out on your own occasionally?
Vera (*she starts arranging the tea-things*) Not to speak of.
Pam Still, I'd have thought it would have been very useful. Shopping, things like that.
Vera Oh no. It's quicker to walk really. And then there's the parking and all that. It's very bad these days trying to park. Dreadful. (*Slight pause*) And then, well really I found I didn't really enjoy driving really. I used to get so tense, you know. All the other traffic and, er, I couldn't seem—well, I'm not a very good driver. Dennis always said I couldn't concentrate. He used to hate driving with me. I mean, he didn't show it. He used to laugh about it but I knew he hated it really. And I just seemed to get worse and worse at it. So I gave up eventually. I think I'm a born pedestrian. That's what Dennis said. All thumbs, you know. (*Pause*) Would you like the car? I mean, supposing you wanted to buy it, would you like it?
Pam Yes. Yes, I would.
Vera Well, why don't you? I mean, if it's the price I'm sure I can get Dennis to—I'm sure I could. It's better than having it stuck in the garage there.
Pam I don't think I could even afford to pay for the petrol.

Vera I expect Neil could though.
Pam Oh yes, Neil could.
Vera Well ...
Pam But then if Neil bought it, it wouldn't be mine would it? It would be Neil's.
Vera Well, I suppose so. Technically.
Pam Really it would. When I get a car, I'll buy it.
Vera I can't say I can really see the difference. Still. Did you work before you were married?
Pam Yes. I was a secretary. Then a supervisor.
Vera Oh really.
Pam I was in charge of twenty-five girls at one time.
Vera Twenty-five. Goodness.
Pam I was the youngest supervisor they ever appointed. Then I was expecting Darren. I planned to go straight back to work as soon as I'd had him but it didn't work out like that.
Vera No, well your priorities change, don't they.
Pam Yes.
Vera You could probably go back now though, couldn't you? If only part time.
Pam I'm not sure that going back to supervise a typing pool is really worth the effort. Even supposing they'd have me.
Vera Well, no. I expect it's very hard work too, isn't it? And as you get older, you ...
Pam Yes.
Vera Not that you're old.
Pam No.
Vera Still.
Pam What I'd really like to do is take a degree course.
Vera A degree? You mean at a university?
Pam And then teach perhaps. I'd like to teach.
Vera Oh, that'd be nice. Teaching would be nice. Younger ones.
Pam No. Older ones.
Vera Oh. Well. I worked in Safeways. We had a really nice lot there. When I was there. Really nice. I don't see them much now. Most of them have got married.
Pam You ought to get a job.
Vera Me? Heavens above.
Pam Do you good.
Vera (*nervously tending the tea-table*) At my age? You must be joking. Anyway I'm far too busy for that. And I'm not qualified. You need qualifications these days. I mean, there was a time when I thought it would be nice to work with old folk, you know, but you need to have qualifications for that. To do it properly. Otherwise you can handle them wrong. I wouldn't want to handle them wrong.
Pam There's nothing to stop you. If you really want to.
Vera No, I suppose not. No more than you really.
Pam No.

Dennis comes from the house followed by Neil

Dennis Here I am then, here I am. Who wants me?
Vera Oh, there you are.
Dennis Here I am. Here comes Taurus the Bull. (*To Pam*) Well?
Pam Hallo.
Dennis No, not hallo. Happy birthday. Say Happy Birthday, Dennis.
Pam Happy birthday, Dennis.
Dennis Thank you.
Vera What about some chairs then, Mr Taurus? We're both standing around here like sore thumbs.
Dennis They're in the garage.
Vera Well, can you get them please.
Dennis Oh dear me, they're not that heavy. (*To Neil*) Dearie me.
Vera Get on with you. I'm glad it's not your birthday every day.
Dennis Ah now, be careful what you say to me. We are two nil down at half time. You're looking at an anxious man.
Vera Oh, sport, sport, sport.
Dennis (*to Neil*) Two nil down.
Neil Really.
Vera Every Saturday afternoon, running, kicking, shooting, jumping. All afternoon.
Dennis You like the wrestling.
Vera I don't like it at all. Great flabby things.
Dennis (*bounding at her ape-like*) Grrrrr.
Vera Oh, get off, Dennis, get off.

Vera moves away below the table. Dennis follows and catches her. Then he goes towards the garage door: he turns back and darts at Pam, who freezes him. He goes round to the garage

Dennis Can you give us a hand, Neil, there's a good lad. (*He tries to open the garage door*)
Neil (*joining Dennis*) Right.
Vera (*picking up the tray*) I'll just see how Mother's managing, then I'll make the tea.
Pam Can I help?
Vera No, no. You stay here. You might get a chair in a month if you're lucky.
Dennis (*struggling vainly with the garage door*) Oh, this damn door.
Vera (*passing them on her way to the kitchen*) Why don't you fix it?
Dennis I'm going to when I've got a minute.
Vera The up-and-under's still jammed as well. The electricity man got trapped in there the other day. He had to crawl through the window.
Dennis That'll teach him to read other people's meters. (*Successfully opening the door*) Ah, that's it.

Dennis and Neil go into the garage. Vera goes into the house

Act I Scene 2   23

During the following, Pam wanders over to the ornamental gate then sits on the little wall below the garage—leaning her head back
I'm really glad you came round today, Neil. I appreciate it very much.

Neil Oh that's ...
Dennis (*moving to the back of the garage and rummaging*) Now where the hell did I put them last year. No, I really appreciate it. And Pam as well. I don't know what it is about birthdays. Some people, you know, they get to our age they start to forget about them but I've always—ever since I was a kid this is—I've always had this special thing about birthdays. (*Finding a chair*) Ah ha. Here's one—here, cop hold of that. (*He gives Neil a chair*) I suppose one of the reasons is that I always had these marvellous birthdays when I was a kid. Marvellous. My Dad, you know. My father, he always made me something. Didn't just buy it. He made it. (*He finds two chairs under the shelves*) He'd go in the garage two or three days before my birthday—(*finding more chairs*)—here's a few more—before my birthday and I wasn't allowed near. I used to hear him sawing away, hammering and that, every evening when he was home while I was lying in bed and I'd think—what's he making this year? What's he going to make for me this year? And then. On the morning he'd produce something I'd never dreamt of like a—well, one year it was a roundabout, you know. Little wooden horses going up and down. All painted. All wood. Beautiful work. Right, that's it. One, two, three, four, five. Five chairs, five of us.

Neil, with three chairs, starts to leave the garage, followed by Dennis with two. Neil stops when Dennis speaks

Oy, before you go. Don't forget to have another look at your car. Two hundred and fifty quid, it's yours.
Neil Well ...
Dennis Nobody else wants it. You won't get it any cheaper. In fact, if you leave it much longer, it'll become a vintage car and start going up again.
Neil Well, I'd buy it, yes. It's Pam, you see. I don't think she—well, she doesn't like the idea of me buying it for some reason.
Dennis Why not? You can afford it, can't you?
Neil Yes, I can afford it. She just doesn't want me to buy it. She wants to buy it.
Dennis (*noticing one of his chairs needs attention, and picking up an oil can*) Well then, give her the money as a present and let her buy it. What's the difference?
Neil No, it's not that. She's—odd like that. (*Suddenly wincing*) Ah ...
Dennis What's the matter?
Neil Nothing. (*Rubbing his shoulder*) Just this slight shoulder pain. I don't know what it is.
Dennis Oh.
Neil No, it's almost as if she resents accepting things from me. See what I mean?
Dennis Lucky fellow. Save yourself some money.
Neil It's as if she's trying to prove something. Only I don't know what it is.

That she can do without me or something. But then again sometime she's—she's ...

Dennis What?

Neil Well, very amorous.

Dennis Really?

Neil At night time. I wake up and she's grabbing on to me. Digging in with her fingernails, you know ...

Dennis That's probably what's wrong with your shoulder.

Neil And scratching. I've got a terrible scratch mark.

Dennis Well, fancy that. She doesn't look the sort.

Neil No.

Dennis What do you do?

Neil Well, I say like—lay off will you. I'm trying to get to sleep. I mean, it's about four in the morning she starts this.

Dennis You need your sleep.

Neil I do. I need eight hours. By the way I think the rumour you heard—about our house being scheduled for demolition—I think it was right. The bloke next door had heard it too.

Dennis Oh. (*He ruminates for a second*) Look, Neil, I've been meaning to ask you—if you're—if you were at some time considering buying this, it occurred to me you must have a bit of spare capital.

Neil Well, a bit yes.

Dennis I was just curious. I hope you don't mind.

Neil No. It was a legacy. Got left it.

Dennis Oh really. Somebody die then?

Neil Yes. My father.

Dennis Ah. What's it doing at the moment?

Neil Well, it's in the bank.

Dennis Ah. Well. Now. It's just that I heard something the other day. Just between ourselves, there's this bloke who's working for this decorating firm and he's decided to set up on his own. And he's looking for capital. Just to get him started.

Neil Ah well ...

Dennis No, he's a good man. I've known him for years. And he's as sharp as they come. He's been slogging his guts out for this lot and finally decided he'd be better on his own. And you know the way these fellows work—I mean, if he leaves, you can bet your bottom dollar he'll take a lot of the best customers with him. But he needs premises, equipment, transport. It all costs money. Now you can say, it'll be a gamble but to my way of thinking, I wouldn't even call it that.

Neil Well, I don't know. I'm not much ...

Dennis No. Quite. What I'm saying is, if you've got, say, for the sake of argument, a thousand pounds to spare ...

Neil Oh, it's more than that.

Dennis More than that, fair enough. But for the sake of this discussion let's say a thousand pounds—now you can put that thousand pounds of yours in the bank and you can literally watch it depreciating even with the interest. By the time you're sixty-five or seventy, you've got the equivalent of thirty

Act I Scene 2

pence. Now this way, looking at it long term, he expands, you expand. His profit's your profit, see what I mean? When you come to sell out, you're laughing.
Neil Well, I suppose it's possible.
Dennis Look, I'm not trying to talk you into anything. Believe me. It's your money but—tell you what, I'll try and arrange for you to meet this fellow. Then you can make up your own mind about him. His name's George Spooner and, as I say, he's a good man. Just see what you think.
Neil OK.
Dennis See what you think. He's a first-class workman. Wonderful. Did you happen to notice our lounge? The lounge in there.
Neil Oh yes, very nice.
Dennis Not the hall. That was somebody else. But he did the lounge. Beautiful work. You just have a look at the way that paper hangs when you next go in there.
Neil I will.
Dennis He's got terrific pride, that's what I like about him. Right, are you fit? (*He claps Neil on the shoulder*)

Neil winces. Dennis apologizes

You take those. I'll take these.
Neil Right.

Neil picks up three chairs and leaves the garage, followed by Dennis with two chairs. Pam rises, meeting them

Pam About time, too.
Dennis Patience. Patience. Seldom found in woman. This looks good. (*He leans one chair against the table, opening the other*) Is Mother coming down?
Pam Vee went to fetch her.
Dennis I didn't think she'd miss out. (*Presenting Pam with a chair*) Madame. (*He sets a chair for Pam up L of the table*)
Pam (*sitting*) Thank you.
Dennis There you are, Cecil. (*He opens the second chair and sets it for Neil L above the table*)
Neil Thanks. (*He hands his three chairs to Dennis, who sets them against the flower tub, then sits where indicated*)
Dennis Oh by the way, while we're alone, just a quick word... Er—how shall I put it? Vee is a bit—well I think looking after Mother and me and all that—she's tended to get a bit—what shall I say?—tensed up. A bit tensed up. Nothing serious but if she—you know—drops anything or spills her tea or slips on her arse—anything like that—er—best to pretend not to notice. Don't laugh or anything.
Pam Why should we laugh?
Dennis I don't know. I mean, if you felt like laughing.
Pam I won't laugh. If somebody falls over, I don't laugh.
Dennis Well, that's fair enough. Fine. No problem. All I'm saying is if you did feel like laughing.
Pam I won't.

Dennis Good. Then you're all right. Neil then.
Neil I wouldn't laugh.
Dennis Great. That just leaves me.
Pam Just leaves you.
Dennis Good. Well. Fine.

Vera brings Marjorie to the door of the house. She is in her coat and carries a rug, a hot water bottle and her handbag

Vera Dennis! Can you take your mother, please?
Marjorie I don't know why we're eating out here, I'm sure. We'll all be in bed tomorrow.

Vera goes in

Dennis springs up and goes to Marjorie's assistance, taking the rug and handbag from her. Neil and Pam rise. Neil sets a chair for her up L of the table

Dennis Here she is. Welcome back to the land of the living.
Marjorie We'll all be in bed with pneumonia tomorrow. (*She stops below the chair set L of the table*)
Dennis For tomorrow we die. (*He passes Marjorie's rug and handbag to Neil*)
Marjorie You'll be laughing at my funeral, you will. I still haven't forgiven you for that kettle. Blowing up in my face.

Dennis laughs

Dennis Right! (*Looking round*) Which way's the wind ... (*He picks up the chair L of the table just as Marjorie is about to sit*)
Neil From over there.
Dennis Right. (*He catches Marjorie by the elbow and moves her round the table to down R of it, setting the chair R of the table*)

Neil opens the fourth chair and sets it L of the table

Pam No, it's not. The wind's coming from here. From round here.
Dennis Right. (*He leaves the chair R of the table and moves Marjorie again, above the table to L of it. He is now hauling her round like a stuffed dummy*)

Vera comes out with the teapot and hot water jug

Dennis sits Marjorie in the chair L of the table

Vera All right, everyone. Sit down now. (*Taking in the scene*) No, Dennis, put her round here. She'll be out of the wind. (*She indicates the far side of the flower tub from the table*) She'll be out of the wind.

Neil opens the last chair and sets it by the flower-tub

Marjorie I can't sit in the wind. I'm sorry.
Vera You're not going to, Mother.

Act I Scene 2

Dennis takes Marjorie and sits her in the chair by the flower-tub, then takes her bag and rug from Neil

Dennis is putting you there. Put her there, Dennis.

Pam sits again L of the table

Dennis I am putting her there.
Vera Yes, put her there. (*She puts the teapot and jug on the table*) All right, then. Sit down, Neil. Help yourself.

Dennis gives Marjorie the handbag and wraps the rug round her

Neil Right. (*He sits above the table, at the R end*)

Dennis has now sat Marjorie at some considerable distance from the table—still in view of everyone but beyond the flower-tub

Vera We'll put the birthday boy here. (*She indicates the chair at the R end of the table and sits above it, L of Neil*)
Dennis Fine. (*He sits at the R end of the table*)*
Vera Oh, it's really nice, isn't it? I never thought we'd be able to.
Neil (*who has been displaying signs of the cold*) Very mild.

Marjorie coughs. Vera reacts

Vera Could you pass me the cups, dear.
Dennis Coming up. (*He half-rises and passes two cups and saucers to Vera*)
Vera (*starting to pour Pam's tea*) Just as it comes for you, Pam?
Pam Please.
Marjorie I'll have to have mine weak.
Vera Yes, you'll get it weak, mother. Just a minute.
Dennis Well, this is a nice spread. Very nice. This you, Vee, or Mother?
Vera (*handing Pam her tea*) I did this. (*Proffering a plate of cucumber sandwiches*) Have a sandwich, Neil.
Neil Er, yes. I'll stick to those if you don't mind.

Vera puts down the plate of cucumber, rather over-anxious. Neil, with a swift reflex gesture, prevents the plate sliding into his lap. Vera offers the paste sandwiches. Neil takes one. Meanwhile, Dennis helps himself to cucumber. Both men help themselves to side plates and napkins. Vera offers a paste sandwich to Pam. Pam takes one. Vera puts down the sandwiches and gives Pam a plate and napkin. Vera resumes pouring tea, this time Neil's cup. As she starts this—

Marjorie (*suddenly*) Where's his cake?
Vera What?
Marjorie Where's Dennis's cake?
Dennis Ah ... (*He rises expectantly*)

Pam and Neil also look more or less expectant

Vera We didn't make one this year, Mother, did we?
Marjorie Dennis always has a cake.

*For plan of seating see p. 50.

Vera Yes, but you've been ill, mother, remember.
Marjorie You could have made him a cake, Vera.

Vera gives Neil his tea

Dennis (*mouthing, sotto-voce across to Marjorie*) It doesn't matter, Mother.
Marjorie (*mouthing likewise*) She could have made you a cake.

Vera becomes aware of this silent conversation. Dennis and Marjorie continue mouthing and gesturing until Dennis becomes aware of Vera's gaze. Vera leans forward to take two more cups. Dennis passes them to her, then sits and gives a final gesture to silence his mother

Vera (*pouring Dennis's tea*) You know what I'm like with cakes. And I can't do all that icing like you do. I just get it all over everything. We should have asked Mrs Mandlesham...
Marjorie You don't need to ask anyone how to ice a cake.
Vera Well, I can't do it.
Pam Nor can I.
Dennis It's all right, mother, it's all right.

Vera gives Dennis his tea. She offers Dennis a cucumber sandwich. He takes one. She offers Neil who declines. She offers Pam

Pam What about your mother?

Pam takes the plate from Vera, rises, and goes and offers the sandwiches to Marjorie. Vera pours her own tea

Marjorie (*unaware of Pam*) Ever since he was a little boy, he's always had his cake. Even when your father was dying, Dennis, I still make you your cake.

Pam gives up proffering the plate, waves it at Marjorie somewhat 'V' sign-like and replaces it on the table, then sits again

Dennis Yes, marvellous they were too, mother. Marvellous.

A long silence. Vera counts the cups, then reaches for the hot water jug. She catches the sugar spoon with her wrist, sending sugar high in the air. Vera attempts to ignore this. The others concentrate their attention elsewhere. Shakily, Vera replenishes the teapot with hot water. The others find this, despite themselves, compulsory viewing. She returns hot water jug to the table, as it happens close to Neil's place. Neil, nervous, shifts his legs. Having safely negotiated this, Vera smiles round. Everyone looks away. Vera reaches for the remaining empty cup and saucer. She rattles it dangerously but places it in front of her. She puts milk in the cup. She starts pouring tea. Marjorie's voice suddenly breaks the silence

Marjorie Remember when you were in the army.

Vera's tea-pouring experiences a hiccup

I parcelled them up and and I sent them to you overseas.

Act I Scene 2

Vera Yes, well, I'm very sorry. (*She rises with the cup, preparing to take it across to Marjorie*)
Marjorie I think the least you could have done, Vera, is to make him a cake. It was really very thoughtless to forget ...

The teacup begins to vibrate uncontrollably in Vera's hand

Vera (*through gritted teeth*) Will someone take this cup, please. Will someone take this cup from me.
Pam (*rising and taking the cup from her*) Here. Here, all right.

Pam takes cup to Marjorie. Vera sits. Neil rises, takes a couple of sandwiches, puts them on a sideplate and takes them over to Marjorie

Neil Would you like a sandwich, Mrs ...

Pam returns and sits

Marjorie Yes, I might as well have a sandwich.

Neil returns and sits. Pause

Seeing as she hasn't made a cake.
Vera (*spilling a cup and saucer*) Oh.

Tea pours all over the table, running down between the slats. Neil and Pam rise hastily. Dennis, still seated, suppresses his mirth

Dennis Oh God.
Pam It's all right. I'll do it. Don't you move, Vee, you'll have it all over everything.
Vera I'm sorry, I ...
Pam No damage.
Neil Can I?
Pam No, please don't.
Neil But if I held this, you could ...
Pam (*sharply*) Please, Neil, leave it to me.
Neil (*angrily*) All right. All right. I was only trying to ... I'll keep my mouth shut in future. (*He takes a sandwich and jams it into his mouth*) Oh.
Dennis Eh?
Neil Cucumber. (*He sits*)
Vera (*in an undertone*) If she says one more word about that bloody cake ...
Pam There we are. All mopped up.
Vera Thank you, Pam.

Pam sits. A silence. Dennis continues his struggle to contain his laughter. Neil has an indigestion spasm. Pam glares at him. Dennis's laughter erupts. He moves away from the table: at length recovers: wipes his eyes: stands surveying the miserable group, smiling

Dennis Well.

Pause

    (*Softly*) Happy birthday to me.
         Happy birthday to me.
         Happy birthday, dear Dennis,
         Happy birth ...

Dennis catches Neil's eye. Neil gently indicates Vera. Dennis darts a look at Vera. He tails off into silence

The Lights fade, and—

        the CURTAIN *falls*

ACT II
Scene 1

The same. October

The lights are on in the garage. Outside it is dark. Dennis has looped a string of coloured electric light bulbs high up near the back wall of the garage. Some of the bulbs are missing from the sockets. He is at present working on his present for his mother. It is a needlework box he has made. He is sanding it with an electric drill with sander attachment. Neil is perched on the bench, a glass of wine in his hand, the bottle nearby. Dennis's glass stands untouched: he is absorbed and hardly listens to Neil's conversation, which anyway is intermittently drowned by the sound of the drill. For a moment Dennis continues to drill, then stops

Neil ... you see, my trouble—Pam's trouble is this. I think we—

Dennis starts drilling, the next is inaudible

—both expect things from each other. Things that the other one is not prepared to give—

Dennis stops drilling

—to the other one. Do you get me?
Dennis Uh-huh.
Neil I suppose it's nature really, isn't it.
Dennis Ah.
Neil You have your opposites—like this. (*He holds up his hands to demonstrate*)

Dennis starts drilling

This is me—that's her. And they attract—

Dennis stops drilling

—like a magnet.

Dennis starts again

Only with people as opposed to magnets, the trouble is with people—

Dennis stops drilling

—they get—demagnetized after a bit. I honestly think Pam and me have reached the end of the road. (*He looks to Dennis for a reaction to this*)

Dennis drills. Neil waits. Dennis stops

I'm saying I think we've reached the end of the road. Pam and me.
Dennis Ah.
Neil It's a terrible thing to say. She's drinking as well, you know. I'm the cause of that.
Dennis Oh, I shouldn't think so. (*Holding up his work*) Does that look level to you?
Neil Looks it. I've reached a crossroads, you see, Dennis.
Dennis (*looking around*) I've mislaid the spirit level.
Neil Suddenly I've got to decide. I've got to make decisions. That's not something that comes very easily to me. Frankly, I find it difficult to make decisions and that truly is what gets Pam. Decide, she says. You decide. She admires strength, Dennis. I think she admires you, actually.
Dennis Oh, does she? That's nice.
Neil Women need a rock, you see. A rock. Trouble is, I'm a bloody marshmallow.

Dennis drills. Neil drones on

Weakness in a man. That's something a woman can never respect. Even today with all this equality, she still expects to find in a man someone she can rely on in a crisis. And if that man doesn't stand up to the test, God help him.

Dennis stops drilling

Dennis (*looking for a piece of sandpaper*) True. True.
Neil Well, you can't say I haven't tried. Anyway, she's given up clawing me to death in the night. (*Pause*) You can't say I haven't tried.
Dennis No.
Neil I mean, this business with George Spooner. That's a start isn't it? I decided that myself. I said, right, if Dennis says he's OK, he's OK.
Dennis He's OK is George Spooner.
Neil So. I didn't even ask her. I just did it. I drew out the money, handed to him and said there you are, George, there's three thousand, five hundred quid. Get on with it. Do your worst.
Dennis You won't be sorry.
Neil I know that. I know that. I liked him. I liked old George.
Dennis The only way you'll lose your money with him is if he drops dead from overwork.
Neil That's what I told Pam.
Dennis What did she say?
Neil She said—she said I was an idiot. You idiot, she said.
Dennis We'll see won't we?
Neil We will. We'll see about that. Did I tell you she's drinking? I can always tell when she's drinking. She gets very—abusive.
Dennis (*sandpapering the edge of the box*) Ah well. Blows over.
Neil Vera's looking better.
Dennis Oh, she is. She's a lot better. She's getting better every day. Once she and Mother can bury the hatchet, we'll be laughing.

Act II Scene 1   33

Neil Are they still ...?
Dennis Not talking at all.
Neil Really.
Dennis Well actually, it's Vera who's not talking to Mother. Mother comes in one door, Vera goes out the other. Ridiculous. Been going on for weeks. I said to them—look, girls, just sit down and have a laugh about it. There's only one life, you know. That's all you've got. One life. Laugh and enjoy it while you can. We'll probably all be dead tomorrow so what's the difference. Do they listen to me? Do they hell. (*Admiring his handiwork*) That's not bad. Not bad at all.
Neil I took your advice by the way. Went to the doctor.
Dennis Oh yes?
Neil Yes.
Dennis And?
Neil He said there was nothing wrong with me.
Dennis Oh good. That must be a relief.
Neil The trouble is can I believe him? Is he saying that genuinely or is he saying there is something wrong with me but it's so wrong that there's no point in telling me?
Dennis Oh, I don't think they do that sort of thing.
Neil They do. I have that on very good authority. They do just that.
Dennis (*looking around for a mallet*) Well, I'd look on the bright side.
Neil Yes, quite right. I had confirmation about our house this morning.
Dennis Oh really.
Neil It's definitely listed for demolition. They reckon in about a year.
Dennis Well, they'll rehouse you.
Neil Oh yes. We'll get rehoused. If we're still together.
Dennis Well, there you are then. Nice new house. Nothing wrong with that.
Neil No. No. True. (*Slight pause*) God, I sometimes feel like jumping off a bridge, Den.
Dennis Oh, come on. Cheer up. It's your birthday. (*He finds the mallet*)
Neil If I wasn't able to come along and talk to you like this, I think—

Dennis picks up the mallet and bangs a loose joint into place

—I think I'd have gone and done away with myself—

Dennis stops hammering

—long before this.
Dennis There we are. (*He shows Neil the workbox*)
Neil Very good.
Dennis Now we'll see who's the joiner in this family. I'll show her.
Neil That your mother's birthday present, is it?
Dennis Yes. Needlework box.
Neil Thanks for the tie by the way. Very nice.
Dennis Oh, glad you liked it. Mother chose it actually.
Neil Ah. Very nice. Good taste.
Dennis Yes she has. Now then, what's next. Happy birthday, by the way. (*He lifts his glass to toast Neil*)

Neil Oh, thank you.
Dennis No, you see, just between ourselves, I'm rigging up a little surprise for Mother. Father always used to do that. He always had some little surprise for her on her birthday. I try to keep up the tradition.
Neil Is that what those are for?
Dennis The lights. Yes. Just a little touch. Had them left over from a barbecue. Look. (*He switches them on by the door. They fail to go on*) Ah. Something wrong. I'll check those. Yes, look some of the bulbs are missing. Steps? Step ladder. (*He finds the step ladder*)
Neil 'Course one of the problems is what to do with Darren.
Dennis When's that?
Neil When Pam and I separate.
Dennis Ah. What did she give you by the way? (*He sets up the step ladder below the bulbs*)
Neil What?
Dennis For your birthday. What did Pam give you?
Neil Oh, I don't think she really had time. She's got her hands full with Darren at the moment.
Dennis There's a square box here somewhere with some coloured bulbs. Can you see if you can see them?
Neil Er... (*He starts to search*)

Pam comes out from the house. She rattles the doorknob of the garage

Pam Hey, you two. Open up.
Dennis Just a minute. Just a minute. (*To Neil*) Quick, sling us that cloth.
Neil Eh?
Dennis To cover this up, quick.
Pam Open up.

Neil throws the cloth to Dennis, who puts it over the box

Dennis Right. Open up.

Neil struggles with the door

Give it a shove. I must fix that. And the other one, come to that. (*He looks for the box of bulbs*)

Neil manages to open the door

Pam (*entering*) What are you doing out here, for heaven's sake?
Dennis Hallo, hallo, here's trouble. Aha, a box of bulbs. These are they. (*He finds the box of bulbs, takes one out and climbs up the step ladder*)
Pam Just what do you think you're doing?
Neil How do you mean?
Pam We're all sat in there twiddling our thumbs waiting for you. What's going on?
Dennis (*plugging in a bulb*) Surprises, surprises.
Neil Just getting things ready, that's all.
Pam And what are we supposed to do in the meanwhile? I mean, there's Vee

Act II Scene 1

and me in the kitchen and Marjorie sitting on her own in the sitting room because Vee won't go in there if she's in there and we're all having a marvellous time. I thought this was supposed to be a birthday party.

Neil Well, don't look at me.
Pam I am looking at you. I want you to come in there and socialize.
Neil All right, all right.
Dennis Could you pass me one of those bulbs, please, from the box?
Neil (*doing so*) I'll be in in a minute.
Pam No, Neil, I mean now. Right now.
Dennis Ta. (*He plugs it in*)
Neil Look I can't at the moment, Pam. I'm ...
Pam I don't care what you're doing, I'm not sitting in there for another half-hour.
Neil Look, don't keep on, Pam, for God's sake. Don't keep on. I've had it up to here.
Dennis And another one, please.
Pam Oh, don't you start that one. You know what happens if you start that one.
Neil I know. I know.
Dennis Bulb, bulb, bulb.
Pam Well, just you remember. You have absolutely no right to complain about anything ever. You've handed over total responsibility to me. You have forfeited any right to say anything ever again.
Neil (*moving to Pam with a threatening gesture*) What the hell are you going on about?
Dennis Another bulb, *s'il vous plaît*.
Pam You have left me to deal with the running of the house entirely. You have left me to bring up your child and you have left me to nurse mother on my own.
Neil I don't know how you can say that.
Pam Because it is true, my love. That is why I can say it.
Neil It isn't true.
Dennis Could somebody steady the steps, please.
Neil (*placing a hand on the steps*) It just isn't true at all.
Pam Of course it's bloody true.
Neil Look don't swear, Pam. Every time you get angry, you start swearing.
Pam I'll do more than bloody swear in a minute if you don't come straight back in there with me this instant. (*As she speaks, she grips the side of the steps in fury*)
Dennis Look, steady, steady, I'll fall off in a minute.
Neil Look, don't do that with the steps, Pam, he'll fall off them.
Pam Serve him right if he did. (*She shakes the steps*)
Dennis Oy. Oy. Do you mind?
Neil Pam, he'll fall off them.

Vera comes from the house and enters the garage

Vera Dennis. Dennis.
Dennis Hallo there.

Vera Dennis, will you please come down at once. Come into the house, go into the sitting room and ask your mother ever so nicely if she would mind turning down the television.
Dennis Can't you ask her yourself, love, I'm a bit ...
Vera I have asked her. Twice I have asked her. She has taken not a blind bit of notice. In fact, I think she's actually turned it up. Do I have to remind you there is a small baby next door.
Dennis Yes, all right. All right.
Vera Who is very probably asleep.
Dennis Would somebody go and turn the television down, please.
Pam I'll go.
Vera No, I want Dennis to go. It's his mother. He can cope with her. I want him to see what she's like.
Dennis How can I go? I'm up a ladder.
Pam It's all right, I'll go.

Pam goes out of the garage and into the house

Vera (*calmer*) What are you doing, Dennis? Will you please tell me what you're doing out here?
Dennis I'm just fixing up a little surprise, that's all. Like I always do.
Vera Surprise?
Dennis For Mother's birthday, love. It's her birthday.
Vera Oh God, don't remind me. "Sixty-seven today. I don't look sixty-seven do I, Dennis? Everyone was amazed when they heard I was sixty-seven."
Dennis (*descending the ladder*) Look, Vee, Vee, Come on. Calm down, love, calm down.
Vera And the butcher, he said—"oh are you sixty-seven, Mrs Crowthorne. I'd never have guessed."
Dennis Vee, listen, it's her birthday. It's only once a year. Now go on. Go in there and give her a smile. That's all she wants. Just a smile. Say—happy birthday, Mother and give her a little drink.
Vera She doesn't need a little drink. She's already downed half a bottle.
Dennis Vera. Now, Vera, for me. Come on, love, for me.
Vera Oh God, Dennis, you just don't—you don't ...
Dennis Now what is it? What don't I do?
Vera You don't ... Look, would you mind very much, Neil.
Neil Eh?
Vera Could you find somewhere else to go just for a minute.
Neil Oh, right.
Dennis He's all right. He's all right.
Vera He's not all right.
Neil It's all right. I'm going.
Dennis Thanks, Neil. Thanks.

Neil goes out of the garage door

Now, Vee, what's the trouble?
Vera It's just ....

Act II Scene 1

Neil (*reappearing in the garage door*) I'll shut the door, shall I?
Dennis Thank you, Neil

Neil closes the door, contemplates whether or not to go into the house, and finally opts to sit on the dustbin

Vera It's just, I think I need help, Dennis.
Dennis How do you mean, help?
Vera From you. I don't think I can manage much longer unless I get your help.
Dennis Help. What way? With Mother? Do you mean with Mother?
Vera Partly. No, not just her. You never seem to be here, Dennis.
Dennis What do you mean? I'm here. I'm home as much as most men. Probably more than most men.
Vera Yes, but then you're out here, aren't you?
Dennis Not all the time.
Vera Most of the time.
Dennis Well, I'm doing things. For the house. I mean, you're welcome to come out here too. There's nothing to stop you if you want to talk. Talk things over.
Vera But we've got a home, Dennis. I spend all day trying to make it nice. I don't want to spend the evening sitting in a garage.
Dennis Oh, come on.
Vera I mean, what's the point of my—doing everything. I mean, what's the point. I need help, Dennis.
Dennis Yes, but don't you see, you're not being clear, Vee. You say help but what sort of help do you mean?
Vera Just help. From you.
Dennis (*putting his arm round her*) Yes, well look, tell you what. When you've got a moment, why don't you sit down, get a bit of paper and just make a little list of all the things you'd like me to help you with. Things you'd like me to do, things that need mending or fixing and then we can talk about them and see what I can do to help. All right?

Vera does not reply

How about that, Vee? All right? Does that suit you?

Vera moves to the door

Vee?

Vera goes slowly out and into the house

Vee. Vee.

Neil rises and sticks his head round the garage door

Neil She's gone inside.
Dennis Oh well. (*He moves the steps*) All this house needs, Neil, is a little bit of understanding and a little bit more of people being able to laugh at themselves. That's all it needs. Sounds simple enough, doesn't it? (*He climbs*

the steps) But when I think of the times I've said it and the times it's ... (*Suddenly, loudly*) Steady the ladder.

Neil (*diving for the steps and steadying them*) Sorry.

Dennis Blimey, I nearly went that time. One more bulb.

Neil One more bulb. (*He hands up a bulb*)

Dennis (*plugging it in*) Now, I'm going to need you for the cake, Neil.

Neil Cake?

Dennis This is what happens. I want you, if you would, to wait in the kitchen. I've hidden Mother's cake on the top of the shelf over the fridge. It's in a big maroon tin. Now, I'll call Mother out here. (*He climbs down the steps*) As soon as she's through the kitchen, out with the cake and light the candles. She walks in here—(*demonstrating, going outside the garage then turning and coming back through the door*)—you see, like this. (*He runs and crouches down by the car driver's door*) I'll be hiding here, you see. Now, as soon as she's through the door, I'll give you your signal. That'll be one long blast on the horn. OK? At the same moment, I jump up—(*jumping up and pulling the cloth over the box*)—happy birthday, Mother—and uncover the present. Meanwhile, you have come in behind her with the cake—(*he demonstrates*)—if you like, singing happy birthday, dear Marjorie or something—and if you can manage it, switching on these lights from here, you see? And at the same moment Vee and Pam also come out of hiding. And you just watch Mother's face. It'll be a picture. A real study.

Neil You're very fond of your mother, aren't you.

Dennis Yes, well I suppose I am. I have to admit it. She's got her faults. She's like Vee, you know. She gets a bee in her bonnet about things but you can soon joke her out of it. Easy as that.

Pam enters from the house with a broken glass in a dustpan

Pam Where do you keep your dustbins in this place?

Dennis Round the side there. Just behind you.

Pam Oh yes. (*She lifts the lid and empties the dustpan*)

Dennis Been a mishap?

Pam Just a little one. Only one or two glasses. Nothing serious. (*To Neil*) Hallo, dearest.

Neil You all right?

Dennis starts collecting up rubbish

Pam Fine, dearest, fine.

Neil Right.

Pam I'm getting very hungry. Is there any chance of eating soon?

Dennis Yes, we're nearly all set.

Pam What have you been doing?

Dennis (*putting odd scraps of rubbish into the bulb box*) Never mind. You'll see. Eh, Neil?

Pam As long as you haven't persuaded him to give away any more money.

Neil Look, it was my money.

Pam Oh quite, quite.

Act II Scene 1

Dennis Not unless he still wants to buy the car.
Pam He can't afford it now anyway.
Neil Oh look, Pam, please.
Pam Go to hell.

Neil goes into the house

Dennis (*starting to climb the ladder*) Neil, would you mind . . . Oh, has he gone?
Pam 'Fraid so.
Dennis Oh well, perhaps you wouldn't mind, Pam. I just want to clear a bit of space in here. Could you pass me that box?
Pam This one? (*She picks up the cardboard box*)
Dennis Ta.
Pam You'll really have to do something about those two, you know. (*She hands him the box*)
Dennis Who do you mean? (*He puts the box in the roof*)
Pam Your wife and your mother.
Dennis (*climbing down*) Ah well. It's a traditional problem really, isn't it? Nothing much you can do. They rub along.
Pam They do not rub along.
Dennis (*tidying rubbish*) Oh well, not just at present. No. But these rows happen. You haven't seen us normally, Pam. I can tell you, there were times in the past when we three, we've sat round in there and we've laughed and pulled each other's legs about things. You'd be amazed.
Pam I would. (*Indicating another box*) You want this one?
Dennis If you would, thank you.

Pam bends to pick up the box. She becomes giddy. She stands up and steadies herself

You all right?
Pam Wah. (*She gives him the box*) Yes, fine. You ever going to sell this thing?
Dennis Well, frankly, nobody seems really interested. And then I thought, well, it could be that in a few months Vee might get it into her head to want to start driving again. I mean, the way things are going she might. I mean, in general terms, she's getting better every day.
Pam What exactly was wrong with her?
Dennis (*continuing to collect rubbish*) Oh well, she got these very gloomy depressions. You know. Nothing was right. She got very jittery so she went to see this doctor, psychiatrist, and he said primarily she was just to take it easier. She wasn't to rush at things. And she went on seeing him for a couple of months and then she seemed to be feeling better and she just stopped going. I mean, I think we got the message. All Vee needs is a happy family atmosphere. To feel she has a home around her.
Pam Could be. Good old Dennis.
Dennis Beg your pardon?
Pam (*holding up the bottle of wine*) May I?
Dennis Help yourself. Help yourself.

Pam (*pouring herself some wine*). I must say, you're very resilient. I think I'd have given up years ago.
Dennis Given up what?
Pam Trying to spread jolly cheer.
Dennis Well. Smile costs nothing does it.
Pam True. True. Could you jolly me up, please, Dennis?
Dennis You? You're all right aren't you?
Pam Amazingly enough, no.
Dennis All right. You tell me your problem. I'll sort it out.
Pam Well. Here am I, constantly being reminded by this avalanche of birthdays we all seem to be having that I'm no longer as young as I'd like to be.
Dennis What does that mean, eh? For a start, what's that supposed to mean?
Pam I feel old, Dennis—old, unfulfilled, frustrated, unattractive, dull, washed out, undesirable—you name it. And I've got absolutely nothing to look forward to. How about that to be getting on with?
Dennis Well, for a start you've got your kid. What about your little boy?
Pam He'll soon go. As soon as he's strong enough to walk, he'll be gone.
Dennis Well, there's Neil.
Pam Next.
Dennis Er—no wait. You can't just say that. What about Neil?
Pam I don't really look forward to Neil as much as I used to, Dennis.
Dennis Really?
Pam Really and truly.
Dennis Well, then, I don't know ...
Pam Do you know what it's like, Dennis? To feel undesirable?
Dennis No. Can't say I do.
Pam That's what he's done to me.
Dennis Sorry? Who's this? We're still talking about Neil, are we?
Pam He's made me feel ashamed. Why should I be made to feel ashamed?
Dennis Depends what you've been up to, eh? (*He laughs*)
Pam He hasn't even paid me the compliment of going after another woman. I could accept that—just about. But to be frozen out—as if I was unnatural—some sort of freak—It isn't me, is it? It's him.
Dennis Neil?
Pam There's something wrong with him.
Dennis Health worries, you mean.
Pam That man's destroying me. He is systematically destroying me. I was the youngest supervisor they'd ever had. I had prospects. They told me. Prospects. They were grooming me for something bigger. That's what they told me when I left.
Dennis That a fact?
Pam They had their eye on me. They said so.
Dennis Very good. You must have made an impression—good.
Pam (*moving towards Dennis*) You don't find me undesirable, Dennis, do you?
Dennis Ah, well—now remember—I'm a married man. (*He moves away*)
Pam Presumably you've still got feelings.
Dennis Not if I can help them, I haven't. (*He laughs*) No, you're very attrac-

Act II Scene 1

tive. I mean, I'm perfectly sure—in another life—assuming such a thing existed—that you'd very probably attract me. I'd go so far as to say, I'd probably fancy you.
Pam Then why the hell doesn't Neil?
Dennis What?
Pam Fancy me—or whatever you call it.
Dennis Well—he possibly does. In fact, I'm sure he possibly does. But listen Pam, when you get to our age—you have to slow down. We all do. I mean I would do things ten years ago, I can't do now. I used to be able to play forty-five minutes each way. Football. Down the road there. Couldn't do it now to save my life. Same with you—same with Neil. You need to adjust.
Pam It is age then? You think?
Dennis Probably nothing more than that.

Pam laughs. Dennis laughs

That any help at all?
Pam I'm sorry, Dennis. You're not doing a very good job. I'm still very depressed.
Dennis Well, I don't know. I mean, what do you want? Want me to do a funny dance for you or something?
Pam Oh yes please. Do a funny dance.
Dennis No, I mean seriously. Seriously I can't cheer you up unless you're serious about it.
Pam Perhaps I should have said yes to the car.
Dennis Well, the offer's still open. Two hundred quid.
Pam I can't afford two hundred pence, Dennis. I used to have some money. Quite a lot of money actually. That I'd saved. But now I'm a housewife so I'm not allowed to have any. (*She opens the car door*) And I spent all my money on curtains and pillow-cases and lavatory brushes. (*She gets in the car and sits behind the wheel*) Brrm brrm.
Dennis Runs well. (*He looks through the car window*)
Pam Fasten your seat belts. Start her up, Dennis.
Dennis Haven't got the keys.
Pam Start her up and let's slip away.
Dennis No, that door's still stuck, you see. I really must fix that.
Pam Come on, Dennis, start her up (*She shuts the car door*)
Dennis You can't. Not in the garage. Not with the door shut.
Pam Brrm brrm.
Dennis You all right?
Pam Brrm.
Dennis (*moving to look through the windscreen*) Pam. Pam.
Pam (*loudly*) BRRM.
Dennis Now come on, Pam. Pam.
Pam Brrm—oh. Oh, Dennis.
Dennis What is it?
Pam I think I'm going to be car sick.
Dennis (*alarmed*) Now hold on, hold on. (*Going to open the car door*) Not on the upholstery. I'll help you out. Hang on.

Pam Oh God.
Dennis (*struggling with her*) Come on, you're all right. Come on.

He tries to tug her clear, by pulling her seat belt off over her head. She appears to be tangled with everything, especially the seat belts and the steering wheel. Dennis tugs at her sweater sleeve. Her arm comes out of it

Oh blimey o'reilly. Come on, Pam.

Dennis moves round the car, opens the passenger door, and sits beside Pam

Marjorie comes out of the house in her party frock

Marjorie Now, you can say what you like, Dennis, I am not sitting in there any longer. I want my surprise. Dennis? (*She enters the garage*)
Dennis Oh Mother, look, could you give me a hand.
Marjorie (*seeing Dennis through the windscreen*) Oh Dennis, you naughty boy.
Dennis Mother, please.
Marjorie It's all right, Dennis. It's all right. I've seen nothing. You needn't worry.
Dennis Mother. (*He continues to struggle*)

Marjorie goes out and starts to close the garage door

Vera enters from the house, confronting Marjorie

Marjorie It's all right, Vera, there's no one in there.
Vera What do you mean? Dennis is in there.

The next eleven speeches should be played over-lapping each other

Marjorie No, Dennis is not in there, Vera. And I would prefer you didn't go in.
Dennis Look, will somebody come and help.
Vera I can hear him.
Marjorie I forbid you to go in there, Vera.
Vera Oh, get out of the way.
Marjorie I will not have my son being unjustly accused. (*She steps back to the garage door*)
Vera I said, get out of the way. (*She pushes Marjorie aside, opens the garage door, and goes in*)
Marjorie (*following*) All right. On your own head be it.
Vera Dennis, I ... (*Seeing them*) Oh, I'm sorry I ... (*She turns to go*)
Dennis Vee, will you give me a hand.
Marjorie I told you not to come in. Serve you right. (*She opens her arms to shield Dennis and Pam from Vera*) There are certain things it is best a wife doesn't know about.
Vera You poisonous old woman. You're loving this, aren't you? It's what you've really wanted all along, wasn't it? For Dennis to go off with somebody. To break up my home.

Act II Scene 2

Marjorie I don't know what you're talking about, Vera, you're being most offensive.
Vera You nasty old toad. You've always hated me. You've always wanted my home.
Dennis Now, Vera ...
Marjorie I don't know what's come over you.
Vera Oh, I'd love to—I'd love to sandpaper your rotten face. (*She goes to the bench and picks up the electric drill*)
Marjorie (*screaming and running to the corner of the garage*) Vera. Vera.
Dennis Now, girls, steady. Girls.
Vera (*following, and screaming above the drill, whose cable is too short for her to reach Marjorie*) You sneaky rotten deceitful sly old toad.
Marjorie Now, you stop that. You stop that. Dennis. Help me. (*She starts to climb the step ladder*)

Dennis releases Pam and gets out of the car

Dennis Now, Vee ... (*He approaches Vera cautiously*)

Pam, released, slumps forward onto the steering wheel. The horn blasts loudly and continuously

Now, Vee, I want you to stop that. I want you to put that down.

Vera turns the drill on Dennis, who backs away and becomes entangled in the cable

Vera (*turning back to Marjorie*) Bitch, bitch, bitch.
Marjorie (*from the ladder*) Stop her, Dennis, stop her. Tell her to stop it.

Neil enters from the kitchen bearing the illuminated cake. As he enters the garage, he switches on the lights, bathing the scene in glorious Technicolor

Neil Happy birthday to you
    Happy birthday to you
    Happy birth ...

Neil's voice tails off, as—

the CURTAIN falls

Scene 2

The same. January, a cold clear morning

Vera sits in the garden, in the "sitting area". She is enveloped in a large rug, with just her face showing. After a moment Dennis comes in through the gate. He carries two large supermarket carrier bags. He has on his coat, scarf and gloves. He moves to Vera and puts the bags down

Dennis There. That didn't take long, did it? I think I've got everything we need. Except that soup. I couldn't get your soup, Vee. Had to get another sort. But the man said it was just as good. Just as good. Now, are you sure you're warm enough out here?

Vera (*in a whisper*) Yes.

Dennis Well, as long as you don't die of exposure on us. I'm not having that. See? I could get Mother to bring you out a hot water bottle. I mean, if you insist on sitting out here... Very crowded in town today. Saturday morning, I suppose. (*He crouches down by Vera*) Oh Vee, now this'll interest you. Listen to this. I heard something today. You remember old Spooner? George Spooner, you remember? The man who did our sitting room. Well, guess what happened? He's run off. With his secretary from his office. Drawn out all the money and done a bunk. Left his wife, his business, everything. What about that, eh? Would you credit it. Nobody knows where they've gone. All those poor people with half their wallpaper hanging off. (*He rises*) Eh? Poor old Neil though. There goes his money. Well, we live and learn. Old George Spooner. I'd have laid my life on the line for George Spooner.

Marjorie comes out of the house

Marjorie Dennis! Oh, Dennis, you're back. Did you get on all right?

Dennis I think so, Mother. I can cope with a bit of shopping without falling down, you know.

Marjorie Well, knowing you. How is she?

Dennis She seems all right.

Marjorie As long as she's warm enough. If only she'd stay in the house, I'd feel happier. I could keep more of an eye on her. She won't have it. She doesn't like it. She gets so fidgety and restless.

Dennis Well, maybe the fresh air'll help her along.

Marjorie Did you get her soup?

Dennis (*picking up the carrier bag*) Yes, we're well stocked up now.

Marjorie I'll try her with some at lunchtime. She had her rice krispies this morning so she's not doing so badly, are you dear? (*Dennis and Marjorie bend towards Vera*) Would you like to take those through to the kitchen, Dennis?

Dennis Will do. Will do.

Marjorie You must be nearly ready for your lunch.

Dennis I wouldn't say no to that, Mother.

Marjorie I've got you a nice chop.

Dennis Lovely. Yum yum.

Dennis goes into the house

Marjorie Now, you're positive you're warm enough, Vera? (*Tucking her in more securely*) That's it. That's better. Now you just sit there quietly. You've no need to worry, do you hear? Dennis is being taken good care of. I'll see to him. You just look after yourself. We just want to see you get better. You know what Dennis has made for me. He's made me a little table. Little

Act II Scene 2

bedside table. You know, I've always needed one. And he mended my lamp. Wasn't that kind? Are you going to have a little soup for your lunch? Eh? Vera? A little soup? Would you like a little bowl of soup? Oh well, I expect you'll tell us if you want anything. I'll be back in a minute, dear. (*Calling*) Dennis dear, put the kettle on, will you?

Dennis (*off*) Just a sec. Front door.
Marjorie Oh. Front door. Front door, Vera. I wonder who that can be.

Marjorie heads towards the house

Dennis emerges with Pam and Neil

Dennis Guess who? Guess who then?
Marjorie Well, fancy that. Hallo there.
Neil Hallo.
Pam 'llo.
Marjorie We haven't seen you for ages, have we?
Neil No, no.
Marjorie Haven't been avoiding us, have you?
Neil No, no. Not really. We just—er ...
Marjorie How's your mother?
Neil Much the same.
Marjorie That's good. Have you come to see the patient?
Pam If we could.
Marjorie She's just round there in the sun. I'll make us a cup of coffee, shall I, Dennis?
Dennis Lovely. Lovely, Mother.
Marjorie Won't be a moment.

Marjorie goes into the house

Dennis Well, this is nice. Nice surprise.
Neil Well, we were ... We thought we'd ...
Pam How's Vee?
Dennis Well, in point of fact, she's a lot better. She's making giant strides. The doctor's delighted. He's over the moon about her. Here we are, Vee. Vee love, look who's come to see you. Pam and Neil, Vee. Come to see you.
Pam Hallo, Vee.
Neil Hallo.

Vera looks at them blankly. They stand round her

Dennis Say hallo, Vee. Say hallo. Hallo.
Vera (*faintly*) 'llo.
Dennis There you are, you see. There you are.
Neil Well, that is progress.
Dennis Certainly is. I mean, last time you saw her, I don't honestly, to be absolutely frank, think she knew who you were. So you see, she's coming along.

Neil Oh yes.

Dennis I mean, yesterday was a break-through. An absolute break-through. She had, what—two good full bowls of soup. Now, that means her appetite is returning which is a very good sign. Two good bowls she had.

Pam Is she all right out here? It's quite cold.

Dennis Ah well. Quite. But when she's in the house, she only frets.

Neil She what?

Dennis Frets. Starts fretting. She seems to be happier out here. I mean, we'd sooner she was in. Than sitting out here exposed to all the elements. I'd be happier. I think we'd all be happier if she was under cover.

Neil I'd have thought she ought to have been under cover.

Dennis Right.

Pam What's the doctor say?

Dennis Well. Go along with her wishes. That's what it boiled down to. Good old rest, that's all she needs. I mean, we talked round the possibility of her, you know, going into a hospital but—er—on balance we decided that the home environment would probably do more for her in the long run. She always hated going away. Hated it. Never enjoyed hotels. That sort of thing. Always at her happiest at home. Home's where she belongs.

Neil Yes, I'd have thought so.

Dennis Of course, at the moment, she's still very much in herself.

Neil Yes, yes.

Dennis The doctor was explaining. A mental injury, which is what Vee's got, is not unlike in many ways a normal physical injury. Like, say, cutting your hand. It takes time to heal. Knit together again, you see. It's the same with her mind. That's what it's doing now. It's knitting together.

Neil Amazing.

Dennis Yes it is. It's amazing.

Neil It's a miracle of engineering, the mind.

Dennis True. True. Mind you, to her advantage she's always been a very fit woman. Physically very strong. She had a good home background, you see. Paid off.

Neil Ah.

Dennis Here, I'll let you into a secret, shall I? You know how old she is today? I know she wouldn't mind me telling you.

Pam Oh, is it her birthday?

Dennis Yes, yes. But have a guess how old. You'll never guess. She's forty-two.

Pam Really?

Neil Good gracious.

Dennis Now, you would have never guessed that, would you?

Neil No.

Pam She's lucky. She's got a very good bone structure.

Dennis She was a lovely girl.

Neil Must have been.

Pam (*crouching dawn by Vera*) Vera? Vee—Vee ...

Neil Does she say much then?

Dennis Er, no, not really no. She says yes occasionally and no. That sort of

Act II Scene 2

thing. And you can get her to say hallo if you work at it. I mean, she can understand you. She'll understand what we're saying now.
Pam Vee ...
Dennis I wouldn't bother. Pam. I really wouldn't.

Pam rises. Pause. They move away from Vera

Neil. I've just heard about George Spooner.
Neil Oh yes.
Dennis Yes, I'm sorry.
Neil Yes.
Dennis I'm still absolutely amazed, I don't mind saying. I mean, he just didn't look the type did he? Rushing off like that. With his secretary was it?
Neil I understand so, yes.
Dennis Well. They're bound to catch up with him.
Neil Yes.
Dennis Bound to in the end. I suppose you'll have dropped a bit then?
Neil No. I dropped the lot actually.
Dennis Ah. Well, it seems like Pam was right for once. Eh, Pam?
Pam Nothing to do with me.
Dennis No, you could really have knocked me down with a ... George Spooner. But you know the most unbelievable thing of all—what I really can't understand. He was a Capricorn.
Neil Ah.
Dennis Capricorns just don't do that sort of thing. It's not in their nature.

Pause

(*Laughing*) As a matter of fact—er—talking of rumours, I'd heard that you'd both separated. Shows how much you can rely on rumours. Don't know where I heard that.
Pam From your mother probably.
Dennis Oh?
Pam Who got it from mine.
Dennis Ah.
Pam We did separate for about a week.
Dennis Oh, I see.
Pam Yes.
Neil But we're sort of together again now. Temporarily anyway. You see, we felt that Pam needed to get qualified. Before she could really start out on her own. What with Darren and that. So she'll probably be working on her qualifications for a bit.
Dennis You'll need qualifications.
Neil She will.
Dennis What are you planning to do, then?
Pam Well, I was considering public relations.
Dennis Ah.
Neil I thought you said you were going into the prison service.
Pam That was a joke.
Neil Oh.

Dennis laughs. Pause

Dennis (*drawing them aside*) Look—er—just between ourselves, I'm glad you came round actually. I was going to give you a ring. That car of Vee's. You know, the one you were interested in ...
Neil Oh yes?
Dennis Well, Vee obviously won't be up to driving it for quite some time—and, er, well, it's just lying there going to waste really. So I wondered if you'd care to have it. I know Vee would like you to have it.
Neil (*exchanging a glance with Pam*) Well ...
Pam I don't think so, thank you.
Dennis I mean, as a gift, you know.
Pam I don't think we'll be needing a car.
Dennis Oh.
Neil Thanks anyway.
Dennis Well, if you do change your minds ...
Neil Thanks.

Pause

Dennis Hey, guess what I did last Saturday?
Neil What?
Dennis I fixed those garage doors. What about that?
Neil I don't believe it.
Dennis I didn't have much choice. I had Mother after me.
Neil Oh, I see.
Marjorie (*off*) Woo-hoo.
Dennis Oh, there she goes. (*Calling*) All right, Mother.
Neil She's looking well these days.
Dennis Oh, she's on top form at the moment. Wonderful. Sixty-seven, you know.
Neil Very good.

Marjorie emerges from the house with a tray of coffee and small cake covered with a cloth

Marjorie Coffee up.
Dennis (*hurrying to her*) All right, Mother, I'll take them. Are we going to have it out here then? It's a bit chilly.
Marjorie Well, yes it is. But what about the ...
Dennis Oh my word, yes. I nearly forgot. (*He takes the cake off the tray and goes to Pam and Neil*) It's a good job you did come round today, you two. Bearing in mind who's twenty-one today, eh? Old Aquarius here. Look, look, Mother's made her a little cake, see? (*He removes the cover and displays a very small iced cake with a single candle in it*)
Neil Ah.
Marjorie It's only a little one. Just a token.
Dennis No point in doing any more. She wouldn't really appreciate it. It's a good job you remembered, Mother.

Act II Scene 2

Marjorie Somebody's got to remember your wife's birthday.
Dennis Vee. Can you see? Mother's made you a little cake, see? Just to prove we haven't forgotten you.

Dennis puts the cake on Vera's lap. She stares blankly

   I think she knows. I think she does.
Marjorie I don't know how she can sit out in this wind.
Dennis We can't keep her in the house, can we? Wouldn't you like to come back in the warm, Vee? Be tucked up at home, eh? Wouldn't that be nicer?
Vera (*after a pause, softly*) No.

Dennis looks at Marjorie

Marjorie No?
Dennis No. (*To the others*) She's still disoriented, you see.
Marjorie (*handing out the coffee*) Pam.
Pam Thanks.
Marjorie Neil. That's yours. No sugar, is that right?
Neil Ah, thank you.
Marjorie And Dennis. That's sugared, Dennis.
Dennis Thank you, Mum. (*He takes some matches from his pocket and lights the candle on the cake*) Well, happy birthday to Vee, eh?
Pam Vee.
Marjorie / **Neil** } Happy birthday, Vee. { *Speaking together*

Slight pause

Dennis (*singing softly*) Happy birthday to you
      Happy birthday to you

Marjorie joins in. She motions to Neil and Pam who join in, too. Vera's lips move silently with them

      Happy birthday, dear Vera
      Happy birthday to you.

The Lights fade, and—

              the CURTAIN *falls*

FURNITURE AND PROPERTY LIST

ACT I
Scene 1

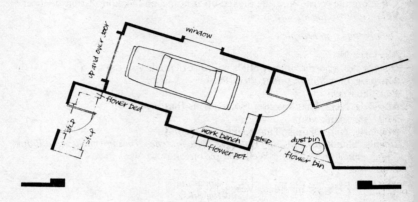

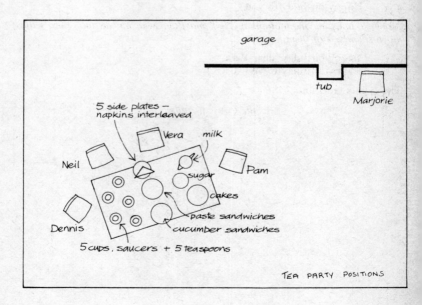

On stage: GARAGE
Car. *Inside it:* seatbelt clipped up, visors up, ignition key in, horn working, radio working, windows open. *Outside it:* aerial raised 6 inches, prop inside bonnet, rubbish on bonnet. *Above it:* wooden box. *Below it:* Valor oil stove with rag on top.
Workbench. *On it:* kettle, kettle lead with wires free, small screwdriver, chisel, rag, vice, various tools. *Under it:* 2 folding chairs, toolbox, electric drill, 2 empty cardboard boxes.
Shelves round wall. *On them:* 2 sheets of sandpaper, mallet, 2 rolls of black linen tape. *On floor:* 3 folding chairs, tea-chests full of junk with cloth on one, box of 6 coloured bulbs, stepladder, assorted rubbish scattered everywhere.

YARD
Dustbin with lid

WALKWAY AND SITTING AREA
Flower-tub with withered plant
Small ornamental trees, withered shrubs
Gate and house door closed
Garage door jammed shut

Off stage: 2 cups of tea, 2 saucers (VERA)

Scene 2

Strike: Kettle, lead, screwdriver, plug
Withered plant from tub
Broken china
Set: Geranium in tub
Garden table
Off stage: Tray with 5 cups, 5 saucers, 5 teaspoons, 5 side plates, 5 paper napkins, sugar bowl, milk jug, plates of white and brown bread sandwiches (PAM)
Plate of biscuits and cakes (VERA)
Rug, hot water bottle, handbag (MARJORIE)
Teapot, hot water jug (VERA)

ACT II

Scene 1

Strike: Tea-things
Garden table
Rug, Hot water bottle, handbag
Geranium
Set: Withered plant in tub
Electric drill (wired up) on workbench
Litter and shavings on garage floor
Needlework box on workbench
String of coloured bulbs across garage wall
Wine bottle and 2 glasses on workbench
Off stage: Dustpan and broken glass (PAM)
Large birthday cake with lighted candles (NEIL)

Scene 2

Strike: Needlework box
Wine bottle and glasses
Dustpan
Electric drill
Set: Folding chair and blanket
Off stage: 2 large carrier bags of shopping (DENNIS)
Tray with 4 mugs of coffee, small cake with one unlit candle (MARJORIE)
Personal: DENNIS: box of matches

LIGHTING PLOT

Property fittings required: 2 overhead lamps in garage, off-stage light in house, dim light outside house door, string of coloured bulbs (Act 1 Scene 2)
Exterior. A garage, pathway and yard.

ACT I Scene 1	Afternoon	
To open:	General effect of winter light	
No cues		
ACT I Scene 2	Afternoon	
To open:	General effect of May afternoon	
Cue 1:	**Dennis's** voice fades singing "Happy Birthday"	(Page 30)
	Fade to Black-out	
ACT II Scene 1	Night	
To open	House and garage lights on. String of coloured bulbs in place but unlit	
Cue 2:	**Neil** switches on coloured lights	(Page 43)
	Snap on string of bulbs	
ACT II Scene 2	Morning	
To open:	General effect of clear cold winter light	
Cue 3:	**All:** "Happy birthday, dear Vera ..."	(Page 49)
	Fade to Black-out	

EFFECTS PLOT
ACT I
Scene 1

Cue 1:	**Dennis:** "Stand by for blast-off." *Car engine turns over*	(Page 5)
Cue 2:	**Dennis:** "... be a little bit cold." *Car engine turns over*	(Page 5)
Cue 3:	**Dennis:** "... She's been standing, you see." *Car engine turns over*	(Page 5)
Cue 4:	**Dennis:** "... come on, you bastard" *Car engine turns over, starts to fire, runs for about 20 seconds, then peters out*	(Page 5)
Cue 5:	**Dennis:** "... It's a good radio." *Radio static*	(Page 6)

Printed in Great Britain by Butler & Tanner Ltd, Frome and London